FULHAM

FOOTBALL CLUB OFFICIAL YEARBOOK 2005/06

Editorial
Patrick Mascall, Tim Beynon, Marc Fiszman, Mark Peters

Design
Simon Sharville, Teb Scott, Ian Bull

Statistics
Karim Biria

Photography
Action Images

Copyright © 2005 Fulham Football Club

Sidan Press, 63-64 Margaret St, London W1W 8SW
Tel: 020 7580 0200
Email: info@sidanpress.com

sidanpress.com

Copyright © 2005 Sidan Press Ltd

Maps redrawn and based on Collins Town and Country series
Copyright © 2005 Bartholomew Ltd
Reproduced by permission of Harpercollins Publishers

Club Directory

Chairman and Directors

Chairman
Mohamed Al Fayed

Business Operations Director
Andy Ambler

Football Business Director
Lee Hoos

Commercial Director
David McNally

Directors
Omar Fayed
Karim Fayed
Mark Collins
Stuart Benson
Ian McLeod

Staff

Team Manager
Chris Coleman

Assistant Manager
Steve Kean

Reserve Team Managers
Ray Lewington & Billy McKinlay

Head of Domestic Scouting
Ewan Chester

International Representative
Craig Brown

Sports Physicians
Chris Bradshaw
Steve Lewis

Head Physiotherapist
Jason Palmer

Academy Organisational Manager
John Murtough

Ladies Team Manager
Marieanne Spacey

Club Secretary
Zoe Ward

Head of Communications
Sarah Brookes

Head of Marketing
Emma Taylor

Head of Ticketing
Harley Evans

Head of Commercial
Olly Dale

Head of Community
Simon Morgan

Stadium Manager
Dave Piggott

Ticket Office Manager
Sandra Coles

Publications Manager
Tim Beynon

Safety Officer
Bob Morrison

Contacts

Fulham Football Club
Motspur Park
New Malden KT3 6PT
Main Tel: 0870 442 1222
Fax (Motspur Park): 020 8336 0514

Ticket Line: 0870 442 1234
Club FFC: 0870 442 1221
Fulham Direct: 0870 442 1223
Community: 0870 442 5432

Club Email: enquiries@fulhamfc.com
www.fulhamfc.com
The ticket office is open to personal callers from 9am till 5pm Monday to Friday, and on match days from 9.30am. Closing times may vary on match days.

Contents

Confirmed sponsors as of July 30, 2005

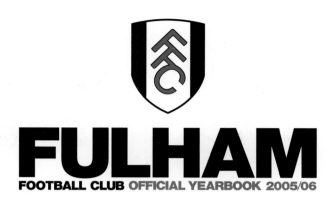

FULHAM

FOOTBALL CLUB OFFICIAL YEARBOOK 2005/06

www.fulhamfc.com
Follow the action all the way to the net!

Chris Coleman

The 2004/05 season has been a massive learning curve from start to finish and has shown us all that we mustn't set our sights too high.

That's not to say we shouldn't be ambitious or competitive – quite the opposite. But the aims we set must be realistic. In an ideal world we'd have liked to have finished 12th. We finished 13th, and apart from a ridiculous decision by a referee up at Middlesbrough, we would have finished 11th. So when you look at it that way, even though the perception is that it was disappointing, we were only one place off where we wanted and expected to finish, and if it wasn't for the Boro game, we'd have finished higher than that.

Strangely enough, I felt more like a manager this year than I did last year, even though the results were indifferent. Because of a combination of our inconsistency, plus a lot of injuries and suspensions, I had to chop and change the side, which meant disappointing a few people. I didn't have to do that so much the season before, and maybe because of that, and because I was new, perhaps they looked at me more like I was a captain still. But I definitely feel I've matured a lot in the last season, given what we've had to come through and the decisions I've had to make. And I actually feel like I'm a much better manager now than I was at the end of the first season, despite the fact that the first season was better as a whole.

I've never doubted myself as to whether I could do this job – I knew I could. Yes, the stress and pressure's always there, and it was this season more than last. But it's made me a better manager, I can tell you. I feel better having come through that experience and having dealt with it.

I've made no secret of the fact that I want to keep this group of players together as much as possible. But, as much as we all want to go forward and have a great season, the most important priority is the long-term future of the Club. So that means operating on a tight budget, which means we've got to be very careful about who we chose to bring in. We all want to sign great players and hang on to the best ones that are already here, and we'll always try and do that. But it has to work within the confines of the budget. There are certain areas that I want to strengthen, but my biggest concern is the age of the squad. I think it's vital that we cut the average age down.

I want to take a new direction in some areas next season and refresh things behind the scenes. Things have remained the same for the last two years and we just want to do a few things differently. We've done a lot of research into it and I'm very confident that we've picked the best programme for Fulham.

So the lesson for the 2005/06 season is to make sure that everyone keeps their feet on the ground. It'll be another long, hard season, no question, and we'll only get through it if we're all together. And that doesn't just mean in the dressing room, but throughout the whole Club – including the fans. When we all pull together, we can be successful.

Season Review 2004/05

FIRE
EXIT
RSARY BAR
THE MULLERY
THIS IS
A NO SMOKING
STAND
D,DL

COME
ON
YOU
WHITES

Manchester City 1
Fulham 1

Fixture Type: **Barclays Premiership** Date: **Saturday August 14 2004** Venue: **City of Manchester Stadium**
Attendance: **44,026** Referee: **MD Messias**

PREMIERSHIP FIXTURE HISTORY

Pl: **3**	Draws: **2**	Wins 😊	◻	◼
Manchester City	1	5	4	0
Fulham	0	2	3	0

STARTING LINE-UPS

🧤 Barton,
McManaman,
Jihai, Macken,
Stuhr-Ellegaard

🧤 McBride,
Pembridge,
Crossley, Goma,
Rehman

STATISTICS

Season	Fixture	🧤	🧤	Fixture	Season
5	5	Shots On Target		2	2
7	7	Shots Off Target		2	2
0	0	Hit Woodwork		0	0
1	1	Caught Offside		7	7
9	9	Corners		4	4
14	14	Fouls		12	12
44%	44%	Possession		56%	56%

Manchester City's struggles at home continued, as visitors Fulham battled back to earn a 1-1 draw on the opening day of the new Premiership season.

It was the same old story for City, who failed to capitalise on total first-half domination and the electrifying forward surges of 22-year-old right winger, Shaun Wright-Phillips. The youngster was in inspirational form, and further enhanced growing claims that he should be included in England coach Sven-Goran Eriksson's immediate plans.

The home side's 28th-minute goal, however, owed more to England past than future. A long throw from summer signing Danny Mills was flicked on at the near-post by Antoine Sibierski, and Robbie Fowler expertly hooked a right-foot shot over his shoulder and into the corner of the net.

Having kept Edwin van der Sar busy prior to their goal, City refused to let up after it. Nicolas Anelka made progress down the right, before teeing up Wright-Phillips for a shot that the Dutchman could only parry. Sniffing a second goal, Fowler went in for the loose ball, but a desperate clearance by Zat Knight saved the day for the visitors.

That escape was to prove vital for Fulham, as they regrouped at half-time and levelled the scores 11 minutes after the interval. Claus Jensen, a new signing from Charlton, clipped over a ball from the right, and hesitancy in the home defence allowed Collins John to swivel and beat David James with the aid of a deflection from 15 yards.

The goal jolted Kevin Keegan's men back to life, and Claudio Reyna saw a fierce 20-yard drive superbly turned away by van der Sar.

The visiting custodian produced another breathtaking save soon after, tipping behind Sibierski's point-blank near-post header from Reyna's free-kick.

Things almost got worse for City nine minutes from time when Andrew Cole produced a neat lay-off to send Jensen clear. However, David James kept his head to snuff out the Dane's weak low finish.

Moritz Volz challenges Antoine Sibierski

LEAGUE STANDINGS

Position (pos before)	W	D	L	F	A	Pts
10 (-) **Man City**	0	1	0	1	1	1
8 (-) **Fulham**	0	1	0	1	1	1

PREMIERSHIP MILESTONE

Andrew Cole, Claus Jensen and Tomasz Radzinski made their first Premiership appearances for Fulham.

PREMIERSHIP MILESTONE

Papa Bouba Diop made his Premiership debut.

"If we want to equal or do better than we did last season, we cannot afford to play like we did in the first half."

Chris Coleman

Collins John celebrates his goal

Fulham 2
Bolton Wanderers 0

Fixture Type: Barclays Premiership Date: **Saturday August 21 2004** Venue: **Craven Cottage**
Attendance: **17,541** Referee: **R Styles**

PREMIERSHIP FIXTURE HISTORY

Pl: **4** Draws: **0**	Wins ⚽ ☐ ■		
Fulham	4	11	1	0
Bolton Wanderers	0	2	4	0

STARTING LINE-UPS

van der Sar
Volz Knight Goma Bocanegra
Diop Jensen Legwinski (c)
John Cole Radzinski

Davies
Pedersen Nolan
Okocha (c) Campo Speed
Gardner Cesar N'Gotty Hunt
Jaaskelainen

⚽ Boa Morte,
McBride,
Pembridge,
Crossley, Pearce

☐ Stelios, Barness,
Hierro, Poole,
Ben, Haim

STATISTICS

Season	Fixture	⚽	☐	Fixture	Season
12	10	Shots On Target	4	15
13	11	Shots Off Target	6	16
2	2	Hit Woodwork	0	0
10	3	Caught Offside	2	2
12	8	Corners	4	13
23	11	Fouls	13	23
56%	56%	Possession	44%	53%

Andrew Cole is mobbed by exuberant team-mates

Andrew Cole netted both goals as Fulham swept aside Bolton on their return to Craven Cottage.

The first came after just five minutes as the summer signing from Blackburn turned home a low Zat Knight drive from close range. The visitors had failed to fully clear a corner, giving the striker the chance to demonstrate his predatory instincts.

A further 77 minutes elapsed before Cole netted his second, and his 200th League goal, drilling home through the legs of Jussi Jaaskelainen after running on to a Claus Jensen pass in the inside-right channel.

In between times, Chris Coleman's side missed a host of opportunities to put the game out of reach. Chance after chance went begging as Cole, Moritz Volz, Sylvain Legwinski and sub Luis Boa Morte all went close to extending the lead.

Moritz Volz shields the ball from Henrik Pedersen

"**Andrew Cole was excellent. He missed a couple of chances, but he's got that arrogance to believe he's going to score in the end.**"

Chris Coleman

For their part, Bolton offered little by way of attacking invention. Jay-Jay Okocha was the only bright spark in a midfield bereft of ideas, and signalled his intentions with a first-minute shot that was well saved by Edwin van der Sar.

The Dutch goalkeeper had little else to do all afternoon, with most of the play taking place inside the visitors' half.

The outstanding Papa Bouba Diop, scorer of the opening goal in the 2002 World Cup, almost netted with a powerful header from a corner. Fellow home debutant Tomasz Radzinski then cut in from the left to fire a right-foot effort narrowly wide.

Before half-time, the Cottagers came even closer. Having latched on to a weak Ivan Campo back-pass, Cole rounded Jaaskelainen before rolling the ball against the foot of the left-hand upright from an acute angle.

Despite introducing Stelios Giannakopoulos and Anthony Barness in the early stages of the second half, Sam Allardyce's side remained unable to get a foothold in the game.

Home substitute Luis Boa Morte twice went close, before Cole relieved any nervous tension with his crisp 82nd-minute finish.

The final whistle saw Craven Cottage bathed in sunlight by the River Thames. After two years in exile at Loftus Road, Fulham's emotional homecoming had gone swimmingly.

Fulham 0
Middlesbrough 2

Fixture Type: **Barclays Premiership** Date: **Wednesday August 25 2004** Venue: **Craven Cottage**
Attendance: **17,759** Referee: **DJ Gallagher**

PREMIERSHIP FIXTURE HISTORY

Pl: **4**	Draws: **0**		Wins ⚽	☐	■
Fulham	3	6	2	0	
Middlesbrough	1	5	5	0	

STARTING LINE-UPS

⚽ McBride, Boa
Morte, Crossley,
Bonnissel,
Pembridge

⚽ Job, Nemeth,
Doriva, Nash,
Cooper

STATISTICS

Season	Fixture ⚽		⚽ Fixture	Season
14	2	Shots On Target	3	16
17	4	Shots Off Target	5	16
2	0	Hit Woodwork	0	0
12	2	Caught Offside	9	21
13	1	Corners	6	17
33	10	Fouls	8	38
52%	46%	Possession	54%	50%

Middlesbrough finally recorded their first victory of the season in an evenly contested clash at Craven Cottage.

Second-half goals from debutant Mark Viduka and substitute Szilard Nemeth saw off the challenge of Fulham, as Steve McClaren's side continued their free-scoring start to the season.

The first period offered little to remember it by, with Edwin van der Sar's smart parry from Viduka and counterpart Mark Schwarzer's save from a Collins John header proving the only moments of note. Boudewijn Zenden posed a constant threat down the left, but all too often failed to deliver a telling final ball.

The same could not be said of fellow Dutchman Jimmy Floyd Hasselbaink in the 54th minute though. Having escaped down the right, the ex-Chelsea man looked up before driving in a low cross that his new strike-partner Viduka steered home from close range. Many people had wondered how this temperamental pairing would get on, with this goal proving a very encouraging sign for Middlesbrough fans.

The Cottagers tried in vain to get back in the game, Tomasz Radzinski just missing out on a cross from Carlos Bocanegra, as Brian McBride and Luis Boa Morte were introduced to supplement the attack.

However, it was a Middlesbrough substitute who ultimately sealed the contest. Having been on the field just two minutes, Slovakian Nemeth bundled home Franck Queudrue's 79th-minute cross at the back post.

That strike served to emphasise just how many options in attack McClaren now has at his disposal. Coupled with a traditionally strong defensive unit, which kept its first clean sheet of the season in this game, the Teesside club look well-set for a productive campaign.

It is difficult to say the same for Chris Coleman's side. Denmark international Claus Jensen looked to be the only player capable of unlocking a Premiership defence, while both Radzinski and John looked uncomfortable playing in wide areas.

Claus Jensen gets the better of Ray Parlour

EVENT LINE

HALF TIME 0 - 0

54	⚽	Viduka (Open Play)
62	🔄	**John (Off) McBride (On)**
71	🔄	Viduka (Off) Job (On)
71	🟨	Zenden (Ung.Conduct)
74	🔄	**Diop (Off) Boa Morte (On)**
77	🔄	Mendieta (Off) Nemeth (On)
79	⚽	Nemeth (Open Play)
89	🔄	Boateng (Off) Doriva (On)

FULL TIME 0 - 2

LEAGUE STANDINGS

Position (pos before)	W	D	L	F	A	Pts
8 (4) Fulham	1	1	1	3	3	4
7 (18) Middlesbrough	1	1	1	7	7	4

"We were poor. Middlesbrough were stronger and more determined."

Chris Coleman

Mark Viduka brings the ball under control

Portsmouth 4
Fulham 3

Fixture Type: **Barclays Premiership** Date: **Monday August 30 2004** Venue: **Fratton Park**
Attendance: **19,728** Referee: **B Knight**

PREMIERSHIP FIXTURE HISTORY

Pl: 2 Draws: 1		Wins ⚽	☐	■
Portsmouth	1	5	1	0
Fulham	0	4	6	0

STARTING LINE-UPS

Hislop
Primus   De Zeeuw (c)   Stefanovic   Unsworth
Stone   Quashie   Berger
Berkovic
Fuller   Yakubu

Cole
Boa Morte   Radzinski
Diop   Jensen   Legwinski (c)
Bocanegra   Goma   Knight   Volz
van der Sar

👕 LuaLua, Taylor,
Ashdown, Griffin,
O'Neil

👕 John, McBride,
Crossley,
McKinlay,
Pembridge

STATISTICS

Season	Fixture 👕		👕 Fixture	Season
24	9	Shots On Target	10	24
14	4	Shots Off Target	4	21
0	0	Hit Woodwork	0	2
8	2	Caught Offside	1	13
19	5	Corners	8	21
36	13	Fouls	13	46
48%	44%	Possession	56%	53%

Portsmouth edged out Fulham in a pulsating seven-goal thriller at Fratton Park, with Nigerian striker Aiyegbeni Yakubu helping himself to a hat-trick.

After a patchy opening, the game appeared dead as a contest when the home side netted three times in nine minutes midway through the first half.

Israeli Eyal Berkovic got the ball rolling in the 19th minute, giving Edwin van der Sar no chance with a swerving 20-yard volley after Yakubu's initial effort had been blocked.

Debutant Ricardo Fuller embarked on a determined mazy run to earn a penalty three minutes later. The former Preston striker was tripped by Luis Boa Morte and Yakubu slammed the resulting spot-kick high into the net.

The Nigerian grabbed his second after 28 minutes,

Claus Jensen is felled by Steve Stone

Papa Bouba Diop goes head-to-head with David Unsworth

Time	Event
19	⚽ **Berkovic (Open Play)**
22	⚽ **Yakubu (Penalty)**
28	⚽ **Yakubu (Open Play)**
39	⚽ Cole (Open Play)
41	⚽ Boa Morte (Open Play)
HALF TIME 3 - 2	
68	▯ Legwinski (Ung.Conduct)
68	⇄ Radzinski (Off) John (On)
72	⚽ **Yakubu (Open Play)**
75	⚽ Bocanegra (Indirect Free Kick)
77	▯ Knight (Foul)
79	⇄ **Berkovic (Off) Lua Lua (On)**
86	⇄ **Legwinski (Off) McBride (On)**
88	⇄ **Yakubu (Off) Taylor (On)**
FULL TIME 4 - 3	

LEAGUE STANDINGS

Position (pos before)	W	D	L	F	A	Pts
11 (19) Portsmouth	1	1	1	6	6	4
13 (10) Fulham	1	1	2	6	7	4

PREMIERSHIP MILESTONE

Carlos Bocanegra scored his first Premiership goal.

> **"On the ball we could not be much better than that, but every time they went forward they looked like they were going to score."**
>
> **Chris Coleman**

firing a stunning left-footed drive low across van der Sar from the inside-left channel, having latched on to a Fuller flick-on. At 3-0, even the most pessimistic of Portsmouth supporters must have felt the game was won, but Fulham had other ideas.

Andrew Cole nodded home his third goal of the campaign from Boa Morte's 39th-minute centre from the left, before the pair reversed roles two minutes later as the Portuguese winger beat Shaka Hislop with a low finish from the inside-left channel after collecting the striker's return pass.

The second half continued in harum-scarum fashion, with countless chances at both ends. A miraculous one-handed save from Hislop denied Cole what looked a certain equaliser, and within 60 seconds Harry Redknapp's team had scored a fourth.

Slack defending from a 72nd-minute goal-kick allowed Berkovic to find Yakubu in the area, and the Nigerian tucked the ball home with a minimum of fuss.

That was not the end of the scoring though, as the Cottagers hit back just three minutes later. Carlos Bocanegra lost his marker to nod home Boa Morte's deep free-kick from the left from within the six-yard box.

Despite late chances, there were no further goals. The second period was also notable for an incident in which Fulham full-back Moritz Volz fell into the crowd. Luckily, neither the player nor anyone in the crowd was badly injured.

Fulham 0
Arsenal 3

Fixture Type: **Barclays Premiership** Date: **Saturday September 11 2004** Venue: **Craven Cottage**
Attendance: **21,681** Referee: **MR Halsey**

PREMIERSHIP FIXTURE HISTORY

Pl: **4** Draws: **0**	Wins ⚽	☐	■
Fulham	0	1	7	0
Arsenal	4	8	11	0

STARTING LINE-UPS

van der Sar

Volz — Knight — Pearce — Bocanegra

Diop — Pembridge

Legwinski (c) — Boa Morte

John — Cole

Henry — Bergkamp

Pires — Gilberto — Vieira (c) — Ljungberg

Cole — Cygan — Toure — Lauren

Lehmann

🔴 Radzinski, McBride, Crossley, Goma, McKinlay

⚪ Reyes, Pennant, Fabregas, Almunia, Clichy

STATISTICS

Season	Fixture 🔴		⚪ Fixture	Season
31	7	Shots On Target	7	53
23	2	Shots Off Target	5	23
2	0	Hit Woodwork	0	3
15	2	Caught Offside	5	12
30	9	Corners	4	33
58	12	Fouls	10	49
50%	40%	Possession	60%	60%

Patrick Vieira and Papa Bouba Diop do battle

Arsenal's winning start to the season continued, thanks in no small part to some favourable decisions from referee Mark Halsey.

The official initially awarded Fulham a first-half penalty, following a challenge by Ashley Cole on namesake Andrew, but changed his mind after the reaction of Arsène Wenger's players caused him to consult one of his assistants.

Then, Collins John saw what looked to be a perfectly legal header ruled out for a push, leaving manager Chris Coleman dumbstruck.

The Gunners later took full advantage of their good fortune, as Freddie Ljungberg, a Zat Knight own goal and then José Antonio Reyes secured what on paper looked a comfortable victory.

Arsenal began the more brightly of the two sides, with Knight heading clear a dangerous Dennis Bergkamp cross and Ljungberg unsettling Carlos Bocanegra

Dennis Bergkamp is tracked by Carlos Bocanegra

EVENT LINE

22	⬜	Vieira (Foul)
HALF TIME 0 - 0		
61	🔄	Pires (Off) Reyes (On)
62	⚽	Ljungberg (Open Play)
64	⬜	van der Sar (Dissent)
65	⚽	Knight (Own Goal)
68	⬜	**Legwinski (Foul)**
71	⚽	Reyes (Open Play)
73	🔄	Ljungberg (Off) Pennant (On)
75	🔄	Vieira (Off) Fabregas (On)
76	🔄	**Legwinski (Off) Radzinski (On)**
82	⬜	Fabregas (Ung.Conduct)
83	🔄	**Boa Morte (Off) McBride (On)**
FULL TIME 0 - 3		

LEAGUE STANDINGS

Position (pos before)	W	D	L	F	A	Pts
15 (13) Fulham	1	1	3	6	10	4
1 (1) Arsenal	5	0	0	19	5	15

PREMIERSHIP MILESTONE

21,681
The attendance of 21,681 was a Premiership record at Craven Cottage.

"**To give the penalty and then not give it is incredible. He said that he changed his mind because of the way the players reacted.**"

Chris Coleman on referee Mark Halsey

with several tricky runs. The best chances, however, fell to the home team.

Mark Pembridge's corner ended with the ball being cleared off the line and Luis Boa Morte forced a smart stop from Jens Lehmann against his former club, before Halsey played his pivotal role.

With boos still ringing in his ears, Halsey went some way towards appeasing the angry locals by turning down a strong penalty appeal from the visitors. Moritz Volz, another former Gunner, only made contact with Thierry Henry's calf as he tried to win possession in the box, but the referee was unmoved.

After Lehmann had kept out John with his legs at the start of the second period, Wenger introduced Reyes. The ever-improving youngster's impact was immediate, as within a minute he was involved in the move that resulted in a 62nd-minute opener.

Swedish midfielder Ljungberg slotted Henry's unselfish pass low to the right of Edwin van der Sar, before Knight poked the ball beyond his own goalkeeper three minutes later as he attempted a challenge on the Arsenal goalscorer.

Six minutes later Reyes completed the scoring, slamming Bergkamp's measured pass powerfully across van der Sar with his left foot. In doing so, the starlet maintained his amazing record of having netted in every Premiership match thus far.

West Brom 1
Fulham 1

Fixture Type: Barclays Premiership Date: **Saturday September 18 2004** Venue: **The Hawthorns**
Attendance: **24,128** Referee: **ML Dean**

PREMIERSHIP FIXTURE HISTORY

Pl: **2** Draws: **1**		Wins ⚽	☐	■
West Bromwich Albion	1	2	6	1
Fulham	0	1	8	2

STARTING LINE-UPS

Kuszczak

Purse (c) Gaardsoe

Scimeca Robinson

Johnson Clement

Koumas Greening

Kanu Earnshaw

Cole John

Boa Morte Legwinski (c)

Pembridge Diop

Green Volz

Pearce Knight

van der Sar

🔳 Albrechtsen, Dyer, 🔳 Radzinski,
Gera, Murphy, Crossley, Goma,
Horsfield Malbranque,
 McBride

STATISTICS

Season	Fixture 🔳		🔳 Fixture	Season
27	5	Shots On Target	3	34
26	4	Shots Off Target	6	29
1	1	Hit Woodwork	0	2
24	4	Caught Offside	1	16
44	11	Corners	9	39
78	9	Fouls	10	68
48%	49%	Possession	51%	50%

Having been involved in the infamous "Battle of Bramall Lane" in their 2001/02 promotion season, the Baggies played out a similarly bad-tempered affair against Fulham.

All the action came in an explosive last half-hour, in which there were two goals and three straight red cards. Nwankwo Kanu's 88th-minute leveller, his first for the club, cancelled out Andrew Cole's 72nd-minute strike, while Cole himself joined Papa Bouba Diop and Neil Clement in being sent for an early bath.

The Cottagers had enjoyed some heated battles with West Brom's near-neighbours Birmingham City in recent seasons, and seemed to have mistaken Gary Megson's side for their West Midlands rivals.

In footballing terms, the opening period was very entertaining. Tomasz Kuszczak, making his debut in the Albion goal, nervously parried a Diop header, while

Ian Pearce towers over Nwankwo Kanu

Collins John bravely wins a header

EVENT LINE

6	🟥	Pearce (Foul)
9	🔄	Radzinski (Off) Goma (On)
33	🟨	**Johnson (Foul)**

HALF TIME 0 - 0

46	🔄	**Hall (Off) Sorondo (On)**
53	⚽	**Johnson (Open Play)**
62	🔄	**Goma (Off) Bocanegra (On)**
62	🔄	**McBride (Off) John (On)**
69	⚽	**Riihilahti (Corner)**
72	🔄	**Routledge (Off) Lakis (On)**
74	🔄	**Riihilahti (Off) Kaviedes (On)**
79	🟨	**Bocanegra (Foul)**

FULL TIME 2 - 0

LEAGUE STANDINGS

Position (pos before)	W	D	L	F	A	Pts
19 (20) Crystal Palace	**1**	**2**	**5**	**8**	**14**	**5**
14 (14) Fulham	**2**	**2**	**4**	**8**	**13**	**8**

"We didn't lose because we had 10 men, it was because we were not good enough."

Chris Coleman

Mark Pembridge keeps Ben Watson at bay

Fulham 2
Liverpool 4

Fixture Type: **Barclays Premiership** Date: **Saturday October 16 2004** Venue: **Craven Cottage**
Attendance: **21,884** Referee: **SG Bennett**

PREMIERSHIP FIXTURE HISTORY

Pl: **4** Draws: **0**	Wins	⚽	☐	■
Fulham	1	6	6	2
Liverpool	3	10	6	1

STARTING LINE-UPS

van der Sar

Volz — Knight — Bocanegra — Green

Radzinski — Diop — Pembridge (c) — Boa Morte

Malbranque — McBride

Baros — Cisse

Riise — Garcia

Hamann — Diao

Traore — Josemi

Hyypia (c) — Carragher

Kirkland

John, Crossley, McKinlay, Jensen, Rehman

Alonso, Warnock, Biscan, Dudek, Sinama-Pongolle

STATISTICS

Season	Fixture		Fixture	Season
48	3	Shots On Target	3	50
40	2	Shots Off Target	7	45
2	0	Hit Woodwork	0	0
23	2	Caught Offside	9	27
51	5	Corners	6	40
101	13	Fouls	10	98
48%	48%	Possession	52%	53%

Tomasz Radzinski tries to get away from Djimi Traore

Liverpool recorded their first away win of the Premiership season in the proverbial "game of two halves" at Craven Cottage.

Trailing to a Luis Boa Morte brace at the break, Rafael Benitez changed the face of the game through the introduction of substitute Xabi Alonso. An own goal by Zat Knight and a poacher's finish from Milan Baros levelled the scores, before Josemi saw red. In spite of this setback, Alonso himself and Igor Biscan netted to secure a memorable three points.

The opening period offered little by way of encouragement for the visitors. Fulham dominated proceedings from the first whistle, Mark Pembridge going closest to breaking the deadlock with a long-range drive.

After 24 minutes, the West Londoners got the goal their

Milan Baros is held up by Carlos Bocanegra

football deserved. US international Brian McBride escaped on the right of the area and drilled in a low cross that Boa Morte steered home from inside the six-yard box at the back post.

Six minutes later, the Portuguese wide man slotted home a second. A jinking run from the increasingly influential Steed Malbranque ended with a measured pass that was swept under the advancing Chris Kirkland from 12 yards out in the inside-left channel.

Chris Coleman would have been a happy manager at the break, but just five minutes after the restart it was 2-1. A hopeful long-range effort from Baros would not have troubled Edwin van der Sar, but the ball struck the head of the unfortunate Knight and looped into the top-left corner of the net.

Galvanised by the goal and with Alonso pulling the strings in midfield, Liverpool seized control. After 71 minutes they got their reward, Baros smashing the ball home from close range after Luis Garcia had seen his glancing header kept out by Fulham's Dutch goalkeeper.

Despite the 77th-minute dismissal of Josemi for a second bookable offence, the result of two fouls, Benitez's side went in front courtesy of a deflected Alonso free-kick with 11 minutes remaining.

Fellow substitute Biscan then secured the points in stoppage time with a cultured right-foot finish from 20 yards.

> **"I am very disappointed. If you are 2-0 up in a game, you shouldn't lose it."**
>
> Chris Coleman

Aston Villa 2
Fulham 0

Fixture Type: Barclays Premiership **Date:** Saturday October 23 2004 **Venue:** Villa Park
Attendance: 34,460 **Referee:** P Dowd

PREMIERSHIP FIXTURE HISTORY

Pl: **4**	Draws: **0**		Wins ⚽	◻	◼
Aston Villa		4	10	4	0
Fulham		0	1	4	0

STARTING LINE-UPS

Sorensen

De la Cruz — Delaney — Mellberg (c) — Samuel

Solano — McCann — Hendrie — Whittingham

Angel — Vassell

Cole (c)

Boa Morte — Malbranque

Pembridge — Jensen — Diop

Bocanegra — Pearce — Knight — Volz

van der Sar

🎽 Cole, Davis, Postma, Hitzlsperger, Ridgewell

🎽 Rehman, John, McBride, Crossley, Radzinski

STATISTICS

Season	Fixture 🎽		🎽 Fixture	Season
62	5	Shots On Target	1	49
57	6	Shots Off Target	6	46
3	0	Hit Woodwork	0	2
23	4	Caught Offside	2	25
62	8	Corners	4	55
162	21	Fouls	14	115
48%	54%	Possession	46%	48%

Goals in either half from Nolberto Solano and the in-form Lee Hendrie secured a comfortable victory for Aston Villa.

Not since the end of August had David O'Leary's men tasted Premiership success, but they were rarely troubled by a Fulham side that had also struggled of late. Torrential rain didn't help the quality of the game, as both teams fought against the conditions.

An early injury to Ian Pearce forced Chris Coleman into the introduction of inexperienced youngster Zesh Rehman alongside Zat Knight at the back. The Villans took this as their cue to apply pressure, but were not rewarded until just before the half-hour mark.

After Hendrie had been upended some 25 yards from goal, Peru international Solano stepped up to curl a majestic free-kick over the defensive wall and just inside Edwin van der Sar's post.

The visitors failed to respond before the break, Steed Malbranque missing the target with their only semblance of a chance. In fact, the home side would have moved further in front had it not been for several poor misses from the out-of-sorts Darius Vassell.

The England striker limped off to be replaced by Carlton Cole after 62 minutes, following a spell of improved play from Coleman's charges. Although Thomas Sorensen had remained fairly redundant in the Villa goal, the Cottagers were unlucky not to be awarded a penalty when Claus Jensen's free-kick appeared to strike an arm.

Any pressure was short-lived, however, as the team in claret and blue sealed the game with 15 minutes remaining. Substitute Cole was involved, teeing up Hendrie for another long-range cracker that left van der Sar helpless.

Such memorable strikes seemed out of place in an otherwise uninspiring contest. Fulham seemed to give up after the second goal, while O'Leary handed a run-out to Ballymena-born midfielder Steven Davis.

Carlos Bocanegra gets the better of Steven Davis

EVENT LINE

10	Pearce (Off) Rehman (On)
16	Volz (Foul)
29	**Solano (Direct Free Kick)**
HALF TIME 1 - 0	
62	**Vassell (Off) Cole (On)**
69	Jensen (Off) John (On)
75	**Hendrie (Open Play)**
78	**Whittingham (Off) Davis (On)**
87	**Hendrie (Off) Hitzlsperger (On)**
88	Cole (Off) McBride (On)
FULL TIME 2 - 0	

LEAGUE STANDINGS

Position (pos before)	W	D	L	F	A	Pts
8 (13) Aston Villa	3	5	2	13	12	14
17 (16) Fulham	2	2	6	10	19	8

"This is the biggest test of my managerial career. I'm learning more about management than I did in the whole of last season."

Chris Coleman

Zesh Rehman tries to stop Darius Vassell

Fulham 2
Tottenham Hotspur 0

Fixture Type: **Barclays Premiership** Date: **Saturday October 30 2004** Venue: **Craven Cottage**
Attendance: **21,317** Referee: **AG Wiley**

PREMIERSHIP FIXTURE HISTORY

Pl: 4 Draws: 0	Wins ⚽	☐	■
Fulham	3	7	3	0
Tottenham Hotspur	1	5	5	0

STARTING LINE-UPS

⚽ Radzinski, Flitney, Green, Rosenior, McBride

🚩 Davies, Kanoute, Carrick, Keller, Taricco

STATISTICS

Season	Fixture ⚽		🚩 Fixture	Season
53	4	Shots On Target	1	52
50	4	Shots Off Target	4	63
2	0	Hit Woodwork	0	4
29	4	Caught Offside	11	40
60	5	Corners	4	48
126	11	Fouls	9	143
48%	52%	Possession	48%	46%

A 2-0 victory saw Fulham end a run of three consecutive Premiership defeats, an unwanted statistic that this result passed on to Tottenham.

Goals in each half from Luis Boa Morte and captain Andrew Cole did the damage, as Spurs failed to ignite at any point during the match. Any efforts the visitors did muster were mostly off target, and tended to be the result of lively individual play from Jermain Defoe.

A diabolical first half was punctuated by one moment of real quality after 33 minutes. Home favourite Steed Malbranque collected possession on the left and slipped a perfectly weighted pass into the path of the onrushing Boa Morte, who coolly slotted low past Paul Robinson from 12 yards out.

It was a picture-book goal, and Zat Knight could have doubled the lead soon afterwards when his header from a free-kick was well saved. A low Defoe drive that fizzed narrowly wide when the game was scoreless was all that Jacques Santini's men could point to by way of chances.

Returning midfielder Sean Davis, who left Fulham under acrimonious circumstances during the summer, saw his every touch booed. Unsurprisingly, this resulted in an under-par performance, and Tottenham lost the midfield battle.

Despite not being at their flowing best, the Cottagers were still more than good enough to win this encounter. A one-goal lead is never secure, however, and it came as a relief to most inside the ground when Cole made it 2-0 after 61 minutes.

This time Boa Morte turned from scorer to provider, battling hard for possession on the left and centring for the striker to nod into the right-hand side of the goal from a central position seven yards out.

A team that had managed just six goals in 10 Premiership games was never likely to recover from such a position, and they seldom threatened to beat Mark Crossley during the remainder of the clash.

Andrew Cole celebrates making it 2-0

Moritz Volz grapples with Sean Davis

EVENT LINE

24	▯	Bunjevcevic (Foul)
33	⚽	**Boa Morte (Open Play)**
41	⮀	Brown (Off) Davies (On)

HALF TIME 1 - 0

61	⚽	**Cole (Open Play)**
67	⮀	Ziegler (Off) Kanoute (On)
70	⮀	**John (Off) Radzinski (On)**
83	⮀	Davis (Off) Carrick (On)

FULL TIME 2 - 0

LEAGUE STANDINGS

Position (pos before)	W	D	L	F	A	Pts
15 (17) Fulham	3	2	6	12	19	11
11 (10) Tottenham H	3	4	4	6	8	13

**"We played better than Tottenham and we deserved the three points.
I can't point any fingers when we put in performances like that."**

Chris Coleman

Newcastle United 1
Fulham 4

Fixture Type: **Barclays Premiership** Date: **Sunday November 7 2004** Venue: **St James' Park**
Attendance: **51,118** Referee: **HM Webb**

PREMIERSHIP FIXTURE HISTORY

Pl: **4**	Draws: **1**		Wins ⚫	▢	▩
Newcastle United			2	7	2	0
Fulham			1	6	4	1

STARTING LINE-UPS

Harper

Hughes — O'Brien — Elliott — Bernard

Jenas — Bowyer — Butt — Bellamy

Kluivert — Shearer (c)

Cole (c)
Malbranque
Boa Morte — John
Pembridge — Diop
Bocanegra — Volz
Rehman — Knight
Crossley

⚫ Robert, Ameobi, Caig, Bramble, Johnsen

🟡 Radzinski, McBride, Rosenior, Legwinski, van der Sar

Fulham triumphed 4-1 at St James' Park, largely thanks to the heroics of goalkeeper Mark Crossley.

The visitors' Welsh shot-stopper had an inspired afternoon, saving everything that was thrown at him. Newcastle hit the target on no less than 20 occasions, but only when they had gone 4-0 down did they find the net.

The opening 25 minutes saw almost constant pressure from the home side. Within the first 100 seconds of play, Lee Bowyer worked a neat one-two with Patrick Kluivert, before forcing a fine parry from Crossley. The ball fell invitingly for Craig Bellamy, but he too was denied.

Further saves followed from Bowyer and Robbie Elliott, as the Magpies became more and more frustrated. Then, with 28 minutes played, frustration turned to despair. Having not featured in the game as an attacking force, a quick Fulham break ended with Collins John beating stand-in custodian Steve Harper from the inside-left channel.

Luis Boa Morte celebrates with Andrew Cole

STATISTICS

Season	Fixture	⚫	🟡	Fixture	Season
100	20	Shots On Target		8	61
66	6	Shots Off Target		4	54
4	0	Hit Woodwork		0	2
37	1	Caught Offside		1	30
103	19	Corners		0	60
144	12	Fouls		16	142
51%	54%	Possession		46%	48%

Steed Malbranque enjoys his afternoon at St James' Park

EVENT LINE

28 ⚽ John (Open Play)

45 🟨 Volz (Foul)

HALF TIME 0 - 1

57 🔄 **Hughes (Off) Robert (On)**

57 🔄 John (Off) Radzinski (On)

65 ⚽ Malbranque (Open Play)

68 🔄 **Bernard (Off) Ameobi (On)**

71 ⚽ Malbranque (Penalty)

76 ⚽ Boa Morte (Open Play)

77 ⚽ **Bellamy (Open Play)**

87 🟨 **O'Brien (Foul)**

FULL TIME 1 - 4

LEAGUE STANDINGS

Position (pos before)	W	D	L	F	A	Pts
9 (9) Newcastle Utd	4	4	4	23	23	16
12 (16) Fulham	4	2	6	16	20	14

"The ball bounced for us today, and a few decisions have gone our way. Mark Crossley was fantastic."

Chris Coleman

Newcastle were angry that they had not been awarded a free-kick in the lead-up to the goal, and came agonisingly close to an equaliser before half-time. Holland international Kluivert did everything right, but could only watch in horror as his potential equaliser struck the unsighted Crossley in the face.

Nine of the north-east team's 19 corners were earned in a positive opening to the second period. Yet, despite growing home pressure, it was Chris Coleman's charges who found the net.

With 65 minutes played, Steed Malbranque lashed home Andrew Cole's pass from just outside the area to make it 2-0. Six minutes later, the same player struck again, this time converting from the penalty spot after substitute Tomasz Radzinski had been upended.

Having completely dominated proceedings, Graeme Souness's men now found themselves three goals behind. That margin was briefly extended to four when Luis Boa Morte raced through to clip the ball beyond an advancing Harper after 76 minutes, before Bellamy responded within 60 seconds with a brave header from Bowyer's right-wing cross.

There was still time for one last save from Crossley, as Newcastle were left to reflect on a spectacular defeat.

Fulham 1
Chelsea 4

Fixture Type: Barclays Premiership **Date:** Saturday November 13 2004 Venue: **Craven Cottage**
Attendance: **21,877** Referee: **UD Rennie**

PREMIERSHIP FIXTURE HISTORY

Pl: **4** Draws: **2**		Wins ⚽ ▢ ▪			
Fulham		0	2	4	0
Chelsea		2	6	8	1

STARTING LINE-UPS

Crossley

Knight   Rehman
Volz   Bocanegra
Diop   Pembridge
Radzinski   Boa Morte
Malbranque
Cole (c)

Robben   Gudjohnsen   Duff
Lampard   Makelele   Smertin
Gallas   Terry (c)   Carvalho   Ferreira
Cech

🅑 McBride, van der Sar, Legwinski, Rosenior, Hammond   👕 Tiago, Kezman, Huth, Cudicini, Bridge

STATISTICS

Season	Fixture 🅑		👕 Fixture	Season
63	2	Shots On Target	11	95
59	5	Shots Off Target	5	96
2	0	Hit Woodwork	0	5
30	0	Caught Offside	4	40
61	1	Corners	5	104
155	13	Fouls	13	155
48%	43%	Possession	57%	56%

Papa Bouba Diop unleashes a stunning equaliser

Chelsea continued to set the pace at the top of the Premiership, overwhelming neighbours Fulham 4-1 at Craven Cottage.

José Mourinho's men dominated from start to finish, though they were briefly pegged back at 1-1 by a stunning 57th-minute strike from Papa Bouba Diop. Arjen Robben quickly restored an advantage that had earlier been provided by Frank Lampard, however, and further goals from William Gallas and Tiago sealed the points.

The Stamford Bridge side, and Robben in particular, posed a massive threat in the first period. After Lampard had seen a fine header kept out by Mark Crossley, the Dutch winger took centre stage.

On no less than four occasions in a dazzling 10-minute spell, the former PSV Eindhoven man engineered great chances through his dribbling wizardry. Two high-class

Luis Boa Morte and Damien Duff only have eyes for the ball

EVENT LINE

23	⬜	Makelele (Foul)
33	⚽	Lampard (Indirect Free Kick)
45	⬜	Lampard (Ung.Conduct)
	HALF TIME 0 - 1	
57	⚽	**Diop (Open Play)**
59	⚽	Robben (Open Play)
63	⇄	Smertin (Off) Tiago (On)
72	⇄	**Pembridge (Off) McBride (On)**
73	⚽	Gallas (Indirect Free Kick)
76	⇄	Duff (Off) Kezman (On)
81	⚽	Tiago (Open Play)
83	⇄	Gudjohnsen (Off) Huth (On)
	FULL TIME 1 - 4	

LEAGUE STANDINGS

Position (pos before)	W	D	L	F	A	Pts
13 (12) Fulham	4	2	7	17	24	14
1 (1) Chelsea	10	2	1	21	4	32

PREMIERSHIP MILESTONE

Papa Bouba Diop scored his first Premiership goal.

"I think they are even better than Arsenal, and teams like us are well below the two of them. I think Chelsea are favourites for the title."

Chris Coleman

saves kept the marauding No 16 at bay, before both Alexei Smertin and Eidur Gudjohnsen failed to profit from their colleague's inspired work.

It seemed only a matter of time until the visitors took the lead, and they did in the 33rd minute. A free-kick was rolled to Lampard some 25 yards out, and the England international midfielder struck a venomous drive that swerved into the right-hand side of the net.

Referee Uriah Rennie turned down two strong penalty appeals from the away side in the lead-up to half-time, even booking Lampard for diving, and Fulham took advantage of their good fortune before the hour mark.

Senegal international Diop capitalised on a poor headed clearance to unleash an unsavable volley from distance, somehow bringing his team level. Home joy was short-lived, however, as within two minutes Robben had netted the goal his performance deserved, following another jinking run.

The Cottagers' resistance was broken, and Chelsea grabbed two more goals. Firstly, Gallas nodded in a right-wing free-kick from close range after 73 minutes. Then, Tiago smartly exchanged passes with Robben, before driving home from the inside-left channel nine minutes from time.

In truth, it could have been much worse for Chris Coleman's charges. The home side did not play badly, but were just overrun by opponents at the top of their game.

Everton 1
Fulham 0

Fixture Type: Barclays Premiership Date: **Saturday November 20 2004** Venue: **Goodison Park**
Attendance: **34,763** Referee: **G Poll**

PREMIERSHIP FIXTURE HISTORY

Pl: 4	Draws: 0	Wins ⚽	☐	▉
Everton		4	8	5	1
Fulham		0	2	12	0

STARTING LINE-UPS

Martyn
Hibbert Weir Stubbs (c) Pistone
Carsley
Gravesen Cahill
Osman Kilbane
Bent

Cole (c)
Malbranque
Boa Morte Radzinski
Pembridge Diop
Bocanegra Volz
Rehman Knight
Crossley

👕 Ferguson, Watson, McFadden, Wright, Yobo

👕 Legwinski, McBride, van der Sar, Pearce, Hammond

A second-half goal from substitute Duncan Ferguson earned Everton their sixth 1-0 victory of the season.

The match wasn't a pretty spectacle, though the majority of the Goodison Park crowd didn't let that bother them as they celebrated a win that moved the Toffees closer to both Chelsea and Arsenal in the Premiership table.

David Moyes's men shaded a dire opening period in which industry and commitment were the watchwords. After his acrimonious departure in the summer, Tomasz Radzinski's every touch was greeted with a crescendo of boos.

In truth, this was all either set of fans had to shout about in an insipid opening 20 minutes. Things improved after this, with Tim Cahill heading narrowly over after a fine move down the right involving Leon Osman.

Zesh Rehman climbs above Marcus Bent

STATISTICS

Season	Fixture 👕		👕 Fixture	Season
81	7	Shots On Target	4	67
72	6	Shots Off Target	2	61
3	0	Hit Woodwork	0	2
41	2	Caught Offside	2	32
79	12	Corners	7	68
165	9	Fouls	22	177
50%	55%	Possession	45%	48%

Carlos Bocanegra outpaces Thomas Gravesen

The final five minutes of the half saw a flurry of goalmouth activity. Nigel Martyn did well to keep out a headed flick from Radzinski, while Mark Crossley acrobatically turned over a seven-yard volley from Osman.

While Fulham continued to struggle to find their rhythm after the break, the Merseysiders began to click into gear. Marcus Bent was the catalyst for an improved showing, creating another headed chance for Cahill, and then forcing Crossley into a fine diving save from distance.

The pressure was mounting, with Bent's recently introduced strike partner Ferguson making the all-important breakthrough after 67 minutes. A right-wing corner was helped on by Kevin Kilbane, and the tall Scot stooped to nod the ball home from four yards at the back post.

Unsurprisingly, being behind sparked Chris Coleman's team into life. A comedy of defensive errors presented visiting captain Andrew Cole with two chances to level the scores, but all the striker succeeded in doing was initiating an ultimately fruitless scramble inside the Everton box.

A last-gasp miss by Radzinski was a further lucky escape for Moyes's men, though the Cottagers didn't really deserve anything from this one.

EVENT LINE

39	▢ Diop (Foul)
HALF TIME 0 - 0	
54	⇄ Boa Morte (Off) Legwinski (On)
62	⇄ **Osman (Off) Ferguson (On)**
67	⊙ **Ferguson (Corner)**
81	⇄ Diop (Off) McBride (On)
83	⇄ **Bent (Off) Watson (On)**
88	⇄ **Gravesen (Off) McFadden (On)**
FULL TIME 1 - 0	

LEAGUE STANDINGS

Position (pos before)	W	D	L	F	A	Pts
3 (3) Everton	9	2	3	16	11	29
13 (13) Fulham	4	2	8	17	25	14

"I thought we competed well with Everton. We worked hard and had some decent chances, but at this level you've got to put those chances away."

Chris Coleman

Fulham 0
Blackburn Rovers 2

Fixture Type: Barclays Premiership **Date:** Saturday November 27 2004 **Venue:** Craven Cottage
Attendance: 19,103 Referee: **R Styles**

PREMIERSHIP FIXTURE HISTORY

	Pl: 4	Draws: 0		Wins 😊	☐	◼
Fulham			1	5	4	1
Blackburn Rovers			3	10	6	1

STARTING LINE-UPS

🦅 McBride, van der
Sar, Pearce,
Rosenior,
Hammond

🦅 Thompson,
Matteo,
Enckelman,
Flitcroft,

STATISTICS

Season	Fixture 🦅		🦅 Fixture	Season
73	6	Shots On Target	5	74
67	6	Shots Off Target	13	91
2	0	Hit Woodwork	0	2
35	3	Caught Offside	4	57
74	6	Corners	6	85
186	9	Fouls	13	228
48%	50%	Possession	50%	48%

Blackburn ended a sequence of four draws with a well-deserved 2-0 victory at Craven Cottage.

Goals in each half from Scottish strikers Paul Gallagher and Paul Dickov secured the points, with the latter scoring from the spot after Zat Knight had been dismissed for a second bookable offence when conceding the penalty.

Fulham began the match in a lethargic fashion, Brett Emerton coming within inches of connecting with a dangerous low cross from the right. The warning wasn't heeded, however, as Rovers went in front on 10 minutes.

Again the ball was delivered from the right, but this time Gallagher nipped in to steer home Steven Reid's near-post centre from close range. Nils-Eric Johansson then nearly headed a second, with the Cottagers' defence all at sea.

Having awoken from their slumber, Chris Coleman's side should have drawn level through Tomasz Radzinski. The former Everton forward found himself bearing down on Brad Friedel, yet could only send an effort the wrong side of an upright.

Further chances came and went at both ends, Sylvain Legwinski attempting a spectacular overhead kick, while Reid fired a drive narrowly over.

Having enjoyed the better of the opening period, Mark Hughes's team had to withstand serious pressure after the restart. Andrew Cole fired over, Lucas Neill made a great saving challenge, and Cole then forced a top-class low stop from Friedel with a 65th-minute strike.

With the storm weathered, Rovers went back on the offensive. After Edwin van der Sar had replaced the injured Mark Crossley, events turned very much in the visitors' favour.

With a first-half caution for a tackle from behind already to his name, Knight was shown a second yellow card when conceding a 76th-minute penalty. The defender handled the ball when sliding in on Paul Dickov, and the former Leicester man comfortably converted the resulting spot-kick.

Papa Bouba Diop is too strong for Brett Emerton

"Blackburn wanted to win the game more than us, and I'm not sure that my players are angry enough about losing."

Chris Coleman

Sylvain Legwinski takes no prisoners

Norwich City 0
Fulham 1

Fixture Type: **Barclays Premiership** Date: **Saturday December 4 2004** Venue: **Carrow Road**
Attendance: **23,755** Referee: **AG Wiley**

PREMIERSHIP FIXTURE HISTORY

	Pl: **1** Draws: **0**	Wins ⚽ ⬜ ⬛		
Norwich City	0	0	1	0
Fulham	1	1	3	0

STARTING LINE-UPS

Green

Edworthy Fleming Doherty Drury (c)

Bentley Mulryne Helveg Huckerby

McKenzie Svensson

Cole (c) McBride

Pembridge Malbranque Legwinski

Diop

Bocanegra Rehman Pearce Volz

van der Sar

Safri, Jonson, Ward, Shackell, McVeigh

Knight, Flitney, Rosenior, Radzinski, Hammond

A seventh-minute Andrew Cole goal proved enough to end Norwich's recent mini-revival, as Fulham got back to winning ways.

The Nottingham-born striker rolled the ball low beyond Robert Green from 12 yards, following fluent approach work involving Steed Malbranque and Brian McBride. The finish was as clinical as the move was swift, leaving the keeper with no chance.

Falling behind seemed to affect Nigel Worthington's men, who offered little for the home crowd to cheer in the opening 45 minutes. The Londoners were dominant in midfield, with Malbranque instigating countless dangerous attacks from his position at the head of a diamond.

Wales international Mark Pembridge twice tried his luck from long range, forcing a fine save and firing wide, while Papa Bouba Diop also stung Green's hands from

Steed Malbranque improvises well

STATISTICS

Season	Fixture 👕		👕 Fixture	Season
79	4	Shots On Target	9	82
91	6	Shots Off Target	6	73
3	0	Hit Woodwork	0	2
58	1	Caught Offside	3	38
77	5	Corners	4	78
225	12	Fouls	13	199
47%	49%	Possession	51%	48%

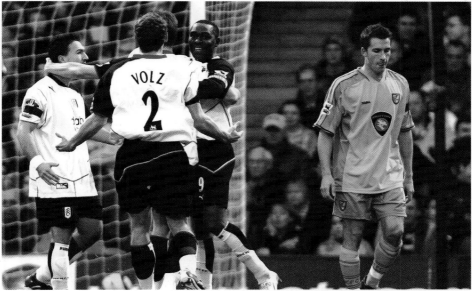

Andrew Cole celebrates his early winner

distance. The Canaries only really threatened on one occasion, when Edwin van der Sar got down well to keep out a low Matthias Svensson effort.

The second half was more evenly contested, as both sides enjoyed periods of dominance without finding the net. Norwich exerted some early pressure, forcing a mistake that ultimately led to a corner.

At the other end, McBride was inches away from connecting with Cole's dangerous cross from the right. That was as close as Fulham came to extending their advantage, though they did carve out several half-chances during the remainder of the game.

The better opportunities fell to a home side desperately in need of an equaliser. Former Tottenham utility man Gary Doherty headed wide from a Darren Huckerby free-kick, before substitute Mattias Jonson did likewise from a left-wing centre.

David Bentley fired over when he should have tested van der Sar, and then squandered another decent opening in stoppage time. Again the on-loan Arsenal man drove high into the crowd, though on this occasion there was no time to try and atone for the miss.

Victory would have seen Norwich climb above the visitors in the Premiership table. As it was, defeat ensured that the gap between the two teams widened to five points.

EVENT LINE

7	⚽ Cole (Open Play)
26	🟨 Volz (Foul)
HALF TIME 0 - 1	
57	🟨 **Helveg (Foul)**
62	🔄 **Mulryne (Off) Safri (On)**
68	🔄 **Svensson (Off) Jonson (On)**
80	🟨 Bocanegra (Foul)
84	🟨 Cole (Dissent)
FULL TIME 0 - 1	

LEAGUE STANDINGS

Position (pos before)	W	D	L	F	A	Pts
19 (19) Norwich C	1	9	6	14	26	12
14 (15) Fulham	5	2	9	18	27	17

PREMIERSHIP MILESTONE

200 Ian Pearce made his 200th Premiership appearance.

"The players really rolled their sleeves up and showed a lot of heart out there."

Chris Coleman

Fulham 1
Manchester United 1

Fixture Type: **Barclays Premiership** Date: **Monday December 13 2004** Venue: **Craven Cottage**
Attendance: **21,940** Referee: **P Dowd**

PREMIERSHIP FIXTURE HISTORY

	Pl: 4	Draws: 3		Wins		
Fulham			0	5	4	0
Manchester United			1	6	9	0

STARTING LINE-UPS

van der Sar

Rosenior Pearce Rehman Bocanegra

Diop

Legwinski Pembridge

Malbranque

Cole (c) McBride

Smith

Rooney Ronaldo

Giggs Scholes

Keane (c)

Heinze Silvestre Ferdinand G.Neville

Carroll

Radzinski, John, Flitney, Knight, Hammond

O'Shea, Howard, Fortune, Fletcher, Bellion

Andrew Cole looks to get the better of Gabriel Heinze

STATISTICS

Season	Fixture			Fixture	Season
85	3	Shots On Target	4		137
80	7	Shots Off Target	12		137
3	1	Hit Woodwork	2		9
39	1	Caught Offside	1		62
84	6	Corners	7		138
215	16	Fouls	14		203
48%	43%	Possession	57%		55%

Fulham's Senegal international Papa Bouba Diop scored a stunning equaliser to earn his side a point against Manchester United and put a serious dent in the Red Devils' title challenge.

United were hoping to move two points closer to Premiership leaders Chelsea after the Blues' 2-2 draw at Highbury, and they looked to be on their way following Alan Smith's first-half goal.

But with just three minutes to play, Diop unleashed a ferocious 25-yard shot to steal a point for Fulham.

It was a particularly gratifying result for the Cottagers given the unavailability of first-choice players Luis Boa Morte, Lee Clark, Claus Jensen, Alain Goma, Mark Crossley and Moritz Volz.

United quickly took control of the first half and it seemed only a matter of time before they found the back of the net.

Tomasz Radzinski is tracked by Roy Keane

"We were delighted to take a point. Some of the football United played was fantastic."

Chris Coleman

Roy Keane went close on 29 minutes, blasting a 25-yard shot against Edwin van der Sar's left-hand post.

Wayne Rooney then rattled the other upright after collecting a Paul Scholes pass wide on the left and cutting inside.

The opener came on 33 minutes, Smith sliding in to steal Cristiano Ronaldo's low cross from Sylvain Legwinski before getting up and slotting home.

The goal was no doubt greeted with dismay at both Highbury and Stamford Bridge, and United nearly had another five minutes later, Keane's belter well saved by van der Sar.

Ronaldo took a dive just before the break as he tried to win an undeserved penalty, but referee Phil Dowd wasn't fooled.

The Portuguese striker then had the final chance of the half, dragging his shot narrowly wide from a good position.

Fulham almost equalised a minute into the second half, Diop's header from a corner spectacularly tipped over by Roy Carroll.

Andrew Cole went close five minutes later, slamming a right-footed shot against the same post that had earlier denied Keane.

Cole then sent a back-header over the bar after Brian McBride had done well to win a high ball on the edge of the box.

Fulham continued to press and were rewarded in the 87th minute, Diop firing home to leave United stunned.

Charlton Athletic 2
Fulham 1

Fixture Type: **Barclays Premiership**   Date: **Monday December 20 2004**   Venue: **The Valley**
Attendance: **26,108**   Referee: **SG Bennett**

PREMIERSHIP FIXTURE HISTORY

		Wins ⚽ ▢ ▪			
Pl: **4**	Draws: **1**				
Charlton Athletic		2	6	6	1
Fulham		1	4	7	0

STARTING LINE-UPS

Kiely

Young   El Karkouri   Fortune   Hreidarsson

Murphy   Kishishev   Holland (c)

Rommedahl   Bartlett   Thomas

McBride   Cole (c)

Malbranque

Pembridge   Legwinski

Diop

Bocanegra   Rehman   Pearce   Rosenior

van der Sar

Jeffers, Konchesky, Euell, Andersen, Hughes

Radzinski, John, Flitney, Volz, Knight

STATISTICS

Season	Fixture 👕		👕 Fixture	Season
79	3	Shots On Target	4	89
66	4	Shots Off Target	3	83
4	2	Hit Woodwork	0	3
57	1	Caught Offside	7	46
72	5	Corners	3	87
239	16	Fouls	16	231
43%	51%	Possession	49%	48%

Charlton moved up to seventh in the Premiership after a 2-1 victory over West London neighbours Fulham.

It was the Addicks' third successive win, a fine response to their previously inconsistent form.

A disappointing Fulham pulled a goal back late in the game to cause some mild panic in the home ranks, but Charlton held on for a deserved victory.

Fulham were tormented all night by 21-year-old winger Jerome Thomas.

The youngster had been on a hot steak of late and was one of the main reasons for Charlton's revival.

Fulham striker Andrew Cole looked to have opened the

Tomasz Radzinski jumps with Luke Young

Carlos Bocanegra makes life difficult for Dennis Rommedahl

scoring on 16 minutes after slotting past Dean Kiely, but the goal was ruled out for offside.

Charlton responded a minute later, Talal El Karkouri rising high to bullet a header from Danny Murphy's corner which Edwin van der Sar did well to keep out.

Thomas moved Charlton ahead on 27 minutes, poking home from seven yards after the Fulham defence had failed to deal with Shaun Bartlett's long-range strike from the right.

Apart from Cole's earlier shot, a Sylvain Legwinski blast from 25 yards was the only effort the Cottagers managed on goal in the first half.

Charlton went close to a second just after the break, El Karkouri hitting the post from the tightest of angles.

Murphy then tried a curling shot which beat van der Sar, only to come back off the foot of an upright.

It seemed only a matter of time before Charlton scored another goal, and on 66 minutes it duly arrived.

The Addicks were awarded a free-kick after Thomas was brought down just outside the area.

Murphy stepped up and curled the ball in towards El Karkouri, whose header just got past van der Sar.

Fulham pressed hard in the final 20 minutes, sending four men up front.

After Cole fired into the side-netting, the Cottagers finally found the back of the net with eight minutes to play, substitute Tomasz Radzinski converting from close range after Charlton had failed to clear a corner.

EVENT LINE

18	⬜	Diop (Dissent)
27	⚽	**Thomas (Indirect Free Kick)**
	HALF TIME 1 - 0	
63	🔄	Malbranque (Off) Radzinski (On)
65	⬜	Rosenior (Foul)
66	⚽	**El Karkouri (Indirect Free Kick)**
73	🔄	Legwinski (Off) John (On)
79	🔄	**Bartlett (Off) Jeffers (On)**
81	⬜	**Kishishev (Foul)**
82	⚽	Radzinski (Corner)
83	🔄	**Rommedahl (Off) Konchesky (On)**
87	🔄	**Thomas (Off) Euell (On)**
	FULL TIME 2 - 1	

LEAGUE STANDINGS

Position (pos before)		W	D	L	F	A	Pts
7 (9)	Charlton Ath	8	3	7	21	28	27
15 (15)	Fulham	5	3	10	20	30	18

"We got a goal at the end, but we didn't deserve anything from the game."

Chris Coleman

Arsenal 2
Fulham 0

Fixture Type: **Barclays Premiership** Date: **Sunday December 26 2004** Venue: **Highbury**
Attendance: **38,047** Referee: **B Knight**

PREMIERSHIP FIXTURE HISTORY

Pl: 4	Draws: 1		Wins ⚽	☐	■
Arsenal		3	8	5	0
Fulham		0	2	5	0

STARTING LINE-UPS

Almunia

Toure   Campbell

Lauren   Clichy

Fabregas   Vieira (c)

Ljungberg   Pires

Bergkamp   Henry

Cole (c)

Radzinski   John

Pembridge   Rehman   Diop

Bocanegra   Knight   Pearce   Volz

van der Sar

⚽ Flamini,
van Persie,
Lehmann,
Senderos,

⚽ McBride,
Crossley,
Fontaine,
Legwinski,
Malbranque

STATISTICS

Season	Fixture	👕		👕	Fixture	Season
151	6	Shots On Target		1	90
87	3	Shots Off Target		1	84
7	1	Hit Woodwork		0	3
37	0	Caught Offside		2	48
105	7	Corners		6	93
207	12	Fouls		9	240
56%	55%	Possession		45%	47%

Carlos Bocanegra puts Freddie Ljungberg under pressure

Arsenal cruised to a comfortable 2-0 win over Fulham at Highbury.

The Gunners were never at their best, but they didn't really need to be against the lacklustre Cottagers.

Fulham had the first real chance on eight minutes, Papa Bouba Diop's header from a left-sided corner cleared off the line by Gael Clichy.

Arsenal responded in the 11th minute, Robert Pires breaking free just inside the Fulham half before cutting inside and firing straight at Edwin van der Sar.

Arsenal opened the scoring a minute later, Thierry Henry collecting from Pires and racing down the left before twisting past Ian Pearce and firing into the right-hand corner for his 16th goal in 19 Premiership matches.

The Gunners continued to control the game, with Patrick Vieira, Pires and Freddie Ljungberg all having opportunities to score.

Robert Pires tries to find a way past Zesh Rehman

EVENT LINE

12	⚽	**Henry (Open Play)**
39	▢	Rehman (Foul)
43	▢	**Vieira (Foul)**
HALF TIME 1 - 0		
66	⇄	Cole (Off) McBride (On)
71	⚽	**Pires (Open Play)**
76	⇄	**Ljungberg (Off) Flamini (On)**
78	⇄	**Bergkamp (Off) van Persie (On)**
81	⇄	Rehman (Off) Malbranque (On)
83	▢	Volz (Foul)
FULL TIME 2 - 0		

LEAGUE STANDINGS

Position (pos before)	W	D	L	F	A	Pts
2 (2) Arsenal	12	5	2	47	22	41
15 (15) Fulham	5	3	11	20	32	18

PREMIERSHIP MILESTONE

50 Moritz Volz made his 50th Premiership appearance.

Henry could have netted a second on 53 minutes if 17-year-old Cesc Fabregas had spotted him speeding down the right flank, but the Spaniard sent the ball to Pires, who was quickly closed down.

Kolo Toure wasted a great chance when he met a corner at the far post, only to send his header high over van der Sar's goal.

Pires went close just before the hour, working his way to the left side of the area before firing a shot from an acute angle which was saved by van der Sar.

Arsenal keeper Manuel Almunia was on hand to deny Tomasz Radzinski in the 65th minute, coming out quickly to collect an attempted lob.

Arsenal thought they'd scored four minutes later when Henry hit a thunderous half-volley that beat van der Sar before slamming against the angle.

But it would only take the Gunners another two minutes to find the back of the net.

Fabregas opened up the Fulham defence with a delightful pass, which Dennis Bergkamp stepped over.

Pires collected the ball in space and moved to the left side of the area before firing past the onrushing keeper.

The rest of the game saw Arsenal playing training ground football as they wound down the clock and collected the points.

> **"You don't need to make things easy for a team with players of the quality that Arsenal have, but we managed to do that for both of their goals."**
>
> Chris Coleman

BARCLAYS PREMIERSHIP

Fulham 2
Birmingham City 3

Fixture Type: **Barclays Premiership** Date: **Tuesday December 28 2004** Venue: **Craven Cottage**
Attendance: **18,706** Referee: **M Clattenburg**

PREMIERSHIP FIXTURE HISTORY

Pl: 3	Draws: 1	Wins ⚽	▢	▮
Fulham		0	2	8	0
Birmingham City		2	4	8	1

STARTING LINE-UPS

van der Sar

Volz — Pearce — Knight — Bocanegra

John — Diop — Legwinski — Radzinski

McBride — Cole (c)

Morrison — Heskey

Clapham — Carter — Savage — Johnson

Tebily — Upson — Cunningham (c) — Melchiot

Taylor (Maik)

Rehman, Malbranque, Hammond, Crossley, Pembridge

Gray, Clemence, Anderton, Vaesen, Taylor (Martin)

STATISTICS

Season	Fixture			Fixture	Season
95	5	Shots On Target		5	91
87	3	Shots Off Target		1	88
3	0	Hit Woodwork		0	4
53	5	Caught Offside		4	62
98	5	Corners		3	100
249	9	Fouls		13	292
47%	47%	Possession		53%	50%

Birmingham's recent revival continued with a good away win at Craven Cottage.

Blues midfielder Robbie Savage, who was being linked with a move to Blackburn Rovers, showed just why the club would hate to lose him.

He was inspirational all afternoon, helping to set up his side's first two goals before rounding things off with a stunning strike of his own.

It was a miserable day for Fulham, who saw Sylvain Legwinski level after Emile Heskey's opener, only for Darren Carter and Savage to reply for Birmingham.

City took the lead on 25 minutes, Clinton Morrison collecting from Savage and playing in Heskey, who worked his way past a defender before firing into the roof of the net from just inside the area.

Fulham equalised against the run of play nine minutes later.

Andrew Cole looks to get in behind the Birmingham defence

Sylvain Legwinski helps the ball on

EVENT LINE

25	⚽	Heskey (Open Play)
34	⚽	**Legwinski (Open Play)**
41	⚽	Carter (Open Play)

HALF TIME 1 - 2

46	⇄	Pearce (Off) Rehman (On)
53	⚽	Savage (Open Play)
56	⇄	McBride (Off) Malbranque (On)
57	⇄	John (Off) Hammond (On)
67	▯	Rehman (Foul)
75	⇄	Heskey (Off) Gray (On)
82	⇄	Morrison (Off) Clemence (On)
86	⇄	Savage (Off) Anderton (On)
90	⚽	**Radzinski (Corner)**

FULL TIME 2 - 3

LEAGUE STANDINGS

Position (pos before)	W	D	L	F	A	Pts
16 (15) Fulham	5	3	12	22	35	18
9 (12) Birmingham C	6	8	6	23	21	26

PREMIERSHIP MILESTONE

150 Sylvain Legwinski netted Fulham's 150th Premiership goal.

"Obviously the players are very disappointed, but we have to get right behind each other and keep on going."

Assistant Manager Steve Kean

Papa Bouba Diop fired a shot that looked to be going wide before it was deflected into the path of Tomasz Radzinski.

The Canadian forward then crossed to Legwinski, who despite falling back while shooting, still managed to find the top corner from 10 yards.

Carter had a chance moments later, but the Blues looked shell-shocked for a time as panic defending set in.

Fulham went close on a couple of occasions before Carter settled the visitors' nerves with a second goal on 41 minutes, coolly slotting past Edwin van der Sar after Heskey had nodded down a cross from Savage.

City could have grabbed another just before the break, Morrison beating the Fulham offside trap to find himself one-on-one with van der Sar, only for the Dutch keeper to make an easy save.

Under-fire Fulham boss Chris Coleman clearly laid into his side at half-time, and they came out flying to start the second period, Andrew Cole forcing a save from Maik Taylor.

But on 53 minutes it was all over, as Savage netted Birmingham's third.

Heskey laid the ball off to the Welshman, who flicked it up with his right foot before unleashing a dipping volley with his left that looped over van der Sar.

Radzinski grabbed a late consolation for Fulham, but the home side were still booed off the pitch.

Fulham 3
Crystal Palace 1

Fixture Type: **Barclays Premiership** Date: **Saturday January 1 2005** Venue: **Craven Cottage**
Attendance: **18,680** Referee: **DJ Gallagher**

PREMIERSHIP FIXTURE HISTORY

	Pl: 1 Draws: 0	Wins		
Fulham	1	3	1	0
Crystal Palace	0	1	3	0

STARTING LINE-UPS

van der Sar

Volz   Knight   Rehman   Bocanegra

Diop   Malbranque   Pembridge

Radzinski   Boa Morte

Cole (c)

Johnson

Lakis   Routledge

Riihilahti   Hughes   Soares

Granville   Popovic (c)   Hall   Butterfield

Kiraly

Rosenior, Clark, John, Crossley, McBride

Torghelle, Andrews, Speroni, Boyce, Leigertwood

Luis Boa Morte shields the ball from Danny Butterfield

STATISTICS

Season	Fixture		Fixture	Season
101	6	Shots On Target	3	82
93	6	Shots Off Target	4	89
3	0	Hit Woodwork	0	5
54	1	Caught Offside	2	53
102	4	Corners	2	101
261	12	Fouls	18	295
47%	50%	Possession	50%	47%

Andrew Cole inspired Fulham to a much-needed victory with two terrific goals at Craven Cottage.

Palace had an early chance, Tom Soares shooting wide in the second minute after running on to a ball over the top from Fitz Hall.

But it was Fulham who would open the scoring two minutes later.

Tomasz Radzinski turned Andy Johnson and picked out Cole in the box, the striker taking one deft touch before burying a right-footed shot beneath Gabor Kiraly.

Fulham then missed a chance for a quick second, Steed Malbranque just failing to get on the end of a pass from Luis Boa Morte.

Wayne Routledge proved a threat all afternoon for the

Andrew Cole is the hero for Fulham

EVENT LINE

4	⚽ Cole (Open Play)
35	⚽ Johnson (Penalty)
	HALF TIME 1 - 1
60	⚽ Cole (Open Play)
64	⇄ Hughes (Off) Leigertwood (On)
65	⇄ Riihilahti (Off) Torghelle (On)
73	⚽ **Radzinski (Open Play)**
76	⇄ **Volz (Off) Rosenior (On)**
79	⇄ Lakis (Off) Andrews (On)
79	☐ Soares (Foul)
81	☐ Butterfield (Foul)
82	⇄ **Malbranque (Off) Clark (On)**
89	⇄ **Boa Morte (Off) John (On)**
90	☐ Knight (Ung.Conduct)
90	☐ Popovic (Foul)
	FULL TIME 3 - 1

Eagles and on 11 minutes his neat run and cross should have set up the equaliser, Tony Popovic heading the ball back across goal, only for Soares to head over from four yards.

Fulham were next to threaten, Malbranque firing wide after Danny Granville could only half-clear a cross from Cole.

Boa Morte then had a chance from Mark Pembridge's corner, but he sent his header wide.

Palace striker Johnson finally came to life on the half-hour mark, his diving header whistling over the bar.

The Eagles won a penalty three minutes later after Fulham keeper Edwin van der Sar clumsily brought down Johnson inside the area.

Referee Dermot Gallagher wasted no time in pointing to the spot, top scorer Johnson stepping up to crack home his 11th of the season.

Johnson almost moved Palace ahead moments later, his acrobatic overhead kick flying just over.

Aki Riihilahti then tested van der Sar with a fierce drive before Radzinski curled in a right-footer which was well saved by Kiraly.

Fulham upped the pace in the second half and reclaimed their lead on the hour, Cole taking a pass from Malbranque on the edge of the box before turning and poking past Kiraly.

Routledge wasted a chance for a quick equaliser, his shot flying well over.

Fulham sealed the win with a third goal on 73 minutes, Malbranque charging down the right before cutting the ball back across the six yard box for Radzinski to slide home.

LEAGUE STANDINGS

Position (pos before)	W	D	L	F	A	Pts
15 (16) Fulham	6	3	12	25	36	21
18 (17) Crystal Palace	3	6	12	21	34	15

"The second half was a great performance in attack. We looked very dangerous."

Chris Coleman

Southampton 3
Fulham 3

Fixture Type: Barclays Premiership Date: **Wednesday January 5 2005**
Venue: **Friends Provident St Mary's Stadium** Attendance: **27,343** Referee: **G Poll**

PREMIERSHIP FIXTURE HISTORY

Pl: **4**	Draws: **3**	Wins ⚽	☐	■
Southampton		1	8	5	0
Fulham		0	6	6	0

STARTING LINE-UPS

Niemi

Telfer · Lundekvam · Davenport · Higginbotham

Fernandes · Delap · Redknapp · A.Svensson

Crouch · Phillips (c)

Cole (c)

Boa Morte · Malbranque · Radzinski
Pembridge · Diop

Bocanegra · Rehman · Knight · Rosenior

van der Sar

⬤ McCann, Jakobsson, Smith, Cranie, Ormerod
⬤ John, McBride, Fontaine, Crossley, Clark

STATISTICS

Season	Fixture ⬤		⬤ Fixture	Season
99	5	Shots On Target	7	108
118	3	Shots Off Target	5	98
2	0	Hit Woodwork	0	3
61	4	Caught Offside	1	55
110	2	Corners	10	112
277	16	Fouls	17	278
48%	44%	Possession	56%	48%

Southampton twice came from behind to earn a point against Fulham.

The six-goal thriller left Harry Redknapp still searching for his first win since taking over as Saints manager six games ago.

Southampton were the first to threaten, Danny Higginbotham's deep cross from the left finding Peter Crouch, whose header was saved by Edwin van der Sar.

On 17 minutes, Papa Bouba Diop almost put through his own net when he sliced the ball over the crossbar following Higginbotham's left-wing cross.

Fulham's Senegalese star made up for that near miss three minutes later, out-jumping Claus Lundekvam to head in Mark Pembridge's precise free-kick from the right.

Southampton quickly responded, scoring twice in the space of nine minutes to turn the game on its head.

Steed Malbranque skips away from Rory Delap

Mark Pembridge is unfazed by the giant Peter Crouch

EVENT LINE

Time	Event
20	⚽ Diop (Indirect Free Kick)
21	⚽ **Phillips (Open Play)**
29	⚽ **Phillips (Open Play)**
42	▢ **Redknapp (Foul)**
43	⚽ Malbranque (Open Play)
44	⇄ **Fernandes (Off) McCann (On)**
HALF TIME 2 - 2	
50	⚽ Radzinski (Open Play)
61	⇄ Radzinski (Off) John (On)
71	⚽ **Rosenior (Own Goal)**
73	▢ **Phillips (Ung.Conduct)**
73	▢ Rehman (Foul)
84	⇄ **Davenport (Off) Jakobsson (On)**
90	▢ Cole (Ung.Conduct)
90	⇄ Cole (Off) McBride (On)
90	⇄ Rosenior (Off) Fontaine (On)
FULL TIME 3 - 3	

Just seconds after Diop's opener, Kevin Phillips headed home Fabrice Fernandes's centre to level matters.

And on 29 minutes, Phillips exchanged passes with strike partner Crouch before turning defender Zat Knight and curling in his seventh of the season.

But just when it looked like Saints would go in ahead at the break, Steed Malbranque equalised for the visitors, tapping home the rebound from eight yards after Luis Boa Morte's angled shot had been saved by Antti Niemi.

Fulham reclaimed the lead five minutes into the second half, Pembridge's through ball playing in Tomasz Radzinski, who made no mistake from 10 yards.

Andrew Cole wasted a chance to move Fulham further ahead three minutes later, shooting well wide from Radzinski's cross.

Cole had a better go on 63 minutes, his right-foot shot turned around the post by Niemi after another good pass from Pembridge.

Pembridge sent the resulting corner in towards substitute Collins John, whose header flew inches over.

Another Pembridge set-piece caused havoc on 70 minutes, Niemi somehow keeping out Knight's shot from three yards.

Fulham were made to pay for their missed opportunities a minute later, Anders Svensson finding space down the right before sending in a low cross which was turned into his own net by Liam Rosenior for 3-3.

Referee Graham Poll denied Saints a late penalty, waving away their appeals after Knight appeared to handle in the box.

LEAGUE STANDINGS

Position (pos before)	W	D	L	F	A	Pts
19 (19) Southampton	2	9	11	22	37	15
15 (16) Fulham		6	4	12	28	39	22

PREMIERSHIP MILESTONE

100 Luis Boa Morte made his 100th Premiership appearance for Fulham.

PREMIERSHIP MILESTONE

Liam Fontaine made his Premiership debut.

"That's the first time we've come back from being behind and got something out of the game for a long time."

Chris Coleman

Fulham 1
West Brom 0

Fixture Type: Barclays Premiership Date: **Sunday January 16 2005** Venue: **Craven Cottage**
Attendance: **16,180** Referee: **P Walton**

PREMIERSHIP FIXTURE HISTORY

	Pl: 2	Draws: 0	Wins ⚫	⬜	⬛
Fulham			2	4	4	0
West Bromwich Albion			0	0	3	0

STARTING LINE-UPS

🧤 Clark, McBride, 👕 Scimeca,
Crossley, Kuszczak,
Rosenior, Koumas, Kanu,
Legwinski Horsfield

STATISTICS

Season	Fixture 🧤		Fixture 👕	Season
112	4	Shots On Target	7	100
102	4	Shots Off Target	2	92
3	0	Hit Woodwork	0	4
58	3	Caught Offside	3	85
119	7	Corners	5	104
288	10	Fouls	11	306
48%	51%	Possession	49%	45%

Fulham midfielder Papa Bouba Diop headed a last-minute winner to heap more misery on West Brom manager Bryan Robson.

The victory moved Fulham seven points clear of the relegation battle.

West Brom went on the attack in the opening minute, Kevin Campbell – signed from Everton on a free transfer during the week – playing in strike partner Robert Earnshaw, whose attempted lob failed to test home keeper Edwin van der Sar.

Luis Boa Morte, who had signed a new contract in the build-up to this clash which would keep him at Craven Cottage until 2008, was a constant thorn in the side of the Albion defence.

He went on two dazzling runs in the first five minutes, ending each one with a cross into the Baggies area which Tomasz Radzinski just failed to convert.

Earnshaw went close in the 10th minute, his shot on the turn saved by van der Sar.

The Dutch keeper then spared the blushes of defender Zat Knight, saving at the feet of livewire Earnshaw after a poor attempted chest-back by his centre-half.

Van der Sar was called into action again moments later, saving a low drive from Ronnie Wallwork.

Boa Morte stole the ball from Darren Purse in the 25th minute, but was unable to find Collins John in the box.

Campbell was denied by van der Sar two minutes later after running on to a through-ball from Purse.

He had another chance moments later, his low effort saved by the keeper.

Boa Morte went close on the stroke of half-time, his flicked header drifting just wide of Russell Hoult's far post.

Despite making the brighter start to the second half, West Brom had to wait until the 59th minute for a clear sight of goal, Earnshaw racing through the home defence before seeing his shot from a tight angle fly narrowly wide.

After Campbell deflected a Wallwork shot just wide, up popped Diop with the late winner, rising unmarked eight yards out to head home Mark Pembridge's corner.

Papa Bouba Diop celebrates his late winner

Brian McBride pressures Ronnie Wallwork

EVENT LINE

22	⮁	**Malbranque (Off) Clark (On)**
37	▢	Greening (Foul)
	HALF TIME 0 - 0	
67	▢	**Boa Morte (Foul)**
70	⮁	Johnson (Off) Scimeca (On)
74	▢	**Bocanegra (Foul)**
79	⮁	**John (Off) McBride (On)**
84	▢	**Clark (Foul)**
90	⚽	**Diop (Corner)**
	FULL TIME 1 - 0	

LEAGUE STANDINGS

Position (pos before)	W	D	L	F	A	Pts
15 (16) Fulham	7	4	12	29	39	25
20 (20) West Brom	1	10	12	17	44	13

"We were fortunate, but we'll take it. Where we are, we need all the points we can get."

Chris Coleman

Birmingham City 1
Fulham 2

Fixture Type: **Barclays Premiership** Date: **Saturday January 22 2005** Venue: **St Andrew's Stadium**
Attendance: **28,512** Referee: **P Dowd**

PREMIERSHIP FIXTURE HISTORY

	Pl: 3 Draws: 2	Wins ⚽	☐	■
Birmingham City	0	3	4	1
Fulham	1	4	7	3

STARTING LINE-UPS

Taylor (Maik)

Cunningham (c)   Taylor (Martin)
Melchiot   Clapham

Diao   Carter
Johnson   Gray

Heskey   Morrison

Cole

Boa Morte   Radzinski
Pembridge   Clark (c)   Diop

Bocanegra   Rehman   Knight   Volz

van der Sar

Blake, Anderton,   McBride, Crossley,
Yorke, Vaesen,   Rosenior,
Tebily   Legwinski, John

Birmingham City slumped to their fourth successive Premiership defeat following Papa Bouba Diop's 83rd-minute header.

It was the third time this season that the Fulham midfielder had scored a late goal, having earned his side a draw against Manchester United and a win over West Brom.

The result capped a bad week for City, who had reluctantly allowed Robbie Savage to join Blackburn a few days before.

There could be little doubt that the Blues missed Savage's industry and enthusiasm in this match.

His replacement, Salif Diao, had a quiet first outing after completing a loan move from Liverpool, appearing out of touch for long spells.

The visitors went close on two occasions in a generally dull opening period.

Maik Taylor had a lucky escape when he took too long over a clearance and the ball was charged down by Luis Boa Morte.

STATISTICS

Season	Fixture 👕		👕 Fixture	Season
112	5	Shots On Target	4	116
99	3	Shots Off Target	3	105
5	0	Hit Woodwork	0	3
72	1	Caught Offside	1	59
121	5	Corners	3	122
339	14	Fouls	10	298
50%	50%	Possession	50%	48%

Lee Clark leads by example

Moritz Volz beats Darren Carter to the ball

With five minutes left in the half, Martin Taylor was forced off the pitch to have a head wound treated.

Fulham quickly looked to capitalise on their temporary man advantage, Andrew Cole firing just wide from a tight angle.

Birmingham's only chance of the half was a Damien Johnson header which flew well wide.

The hosts made a brighter start to the second half and took the lead on 51 minutes, Mario Melchiot sending a deep cross from the right into the middle of the Fulham penalty area where Emile Heskey saw his shot parried by Edwin van der Sar against Moritz Volz and into the back of the net.

Cole quickly responded for Fulham, his angled shot flashing just over.

Robbie Blake came on for Clinton Morrison in the 69th minute and went close with a drive from outside the area after neat work from Heskey.

Fulham plugged away and grabbed the equaliser on 78 minutes, Cole converting a penalty after Boa Morte had been impeded by Johnson.

Four minutes later, the unfortunate Johnson conceded a free-kick in a dangerous position on the left after kicking out at Boa Morte.

Mark Pembridge sent an accurate cross in towards Diop, who rose high above Melchiot and Martin Taylor to head home the winner.

EVENT LINE

	HALF TIME 0 - 0	
51	⚽	**Volz (Own Goal)**
53	▢	Boa Morte (Ung.Conduct)
69	⇄	**Morrison (Off) Blake (On)**
78	⚽	**Cole (Penalty)**
82	▢	**Johnson (Foul)**
83	⇄	**Johnson (Off) Anderton (On)**
83	⚽	Diop (Indirect Free Kick)
84	▢	Diop (Ung.Conduct)
86	⇄	**Taylor Martin (Off) Yorke (On)**
89	⇄	Cole (Off) McBride (On)
90	▢	Bocanegra (Foul)
	FULL TIME 1 - 2	

LEAGUE STANDINGS

Position (pos before)	W	D	L	F	A	Pts
15 (14) Birmingham C	6	8	10	27	30	26
13 (15) Fulham	8	4	12	31	40	28

"A month ago we lost at home to Birmingham, but now we are looking really good."

Chris Coleman

Fulham 1
Aston Villa 1

Fixture Type: **Barclays Premiership** Date: **Wednesday February 2 2005** Venue: **Craven Cottage**
Attendance: **17,624** Referee: **CJ Foy**

PREMIERSHIP FIXTURE HISTORY

	Pl: **4**	Draws: **2**		Wins ⚽	☐	■
Fulham			1	4	5	1
Aston Villa			1	4	9	0

STARTING LINE-UPS

🧤 John, McBride,
Crossley, Goma,
Legwinski

👕 L Moore, Davis,
Djemba-Djemba,
Postma, Laursen

Lee Clark savours his late leveller

It was a tale of missed penalties at Craven Cottage, as Fulham and Aston Villa shared a 1-1 draw.

Colombian Juan Pablo Angel could have had a hat-trick, seeing two spot-kicks saved after he had put his team in front in the 55th minute.

Andrew Cole had also missed with a penalty shortly after Angel's opener, but his captain Lee Clark staved off defeat with a stoppage-time leveller.

The game began at breakneck pace, and Tomasz Radzinski should have tested Thomas Sorensen more severely when presented with a chance inside the opening 30 seconds. Lee Hendrie then fired high and wide for the visitors, as neither side took a grip on proceedings.

A fluent move from the Cottagers deserved a goal, as Luis Boa Morte benefitted from Cole's dummy and exchanged passes with Clark. Unfortunately for the Portuguese international, Sorensen was on hand to repel his right-footed effort.

STATISTICS

Season	Fixture	🥅		👕 Fixture	Season
121	5	Shots On Target	2		130
112	7	Shots Off Target	10		135
3	0	Hit Woodwork	0		3
61	2	Caught Offside	5		70
126	4	Corners	8		146
310	12	Fouls	17		380
48%	48%	Possession	52%		49%

Edwin van der Sar and Collins John celebrate the keeper's penalty save

The remainder of the half offered little by way of noteworthy action. Everything changed soon after the interval, however, as the game exploded back into life.

A startling miss by Hendrie, side-footing Nolberto Solano's inviting cross over the bar, was quickly forgotten as Angel ended a personal goal drought stretching back nearly three months. The striker escaped his marker at the near post to glance Thomas Hitzlsperger's right-wing corner into the net from four yards out.

Shortly afterwards came the first of an incredible three penalty misses. Olof Mellberg was adjudged to have brought down Boa Morte by referee Chris Foy, but Cole dragged his 12-yard effort wide of the post.

As the match reached its final quarter, Angel was presented with an opportunity to seal the points. Moritz Volz was penalised for a challenge on Villa substitute Luke Moore inside the area, though Edwin van der Sar made a terrific save from the spot-kick.

An almost identical scenario played out within the next 10 minutes, Moore winning a penalty, this time after a tackle from Liam Rosenior, and van der Sar denying Angel…again!

With time almost up, the Colombian was made to feel even worse. A deflected Boa Morte drive reared up in the box, and Clark arrived on cue to drill a 15-yard effort into the bottom-right corner.

EVENT LINE

32	▢	De la Cruz (Foul)
HALF TIME 0 - 0		
46	⇄	Cole (Off) Moore L (On)
55	⚽	Angel (Corner)
64	⇄	Hendrie (Off) Davis (On)
68	⇄	**Radzinski (Off) John (On)**
73	⇄	**Cole (Off) McBride (On)**
79	⇄	Solano (Off) Djemba-Djemba (On)
85	▢	**Boa Morte (Foul)**
90	⚽	**Clark (Open Play)**
90	▢	Angel (Ung.Conduct)
90	▢	Davis (Ung.Conduct)
FULL TIME 1 - 1		

LEAGUE STANDINGS

Position (pos before)	W	D	L	F	A	Pts
15 (14) Fulham	8	5	12	32	41	29
11 (11) Aston Villa	8	8	9	28	30	32

> **"We've got a good result on a night when I didn't think it was going to happen for us."**
> Chris Coleman

Liverpool 3
Fulham 1

Fixture Type: **Barclays Premiership** Date: **Saturday February 5 2005** Venue: **Anfield**
Attendance: **43,534** Referee: **R Styles**

PREMIERSHIP FIXTURE HISTORY

Pl: 4	Draws: 2		Wins ⚽	☐	■
Liverpool			2	5	2	0
Fulham			0	1	9	0

STARTING LINE-UPS

Dudek

Finnan Carragher Hyypia Traore

Garcia Gerrard (c) Biscan Riise

Baros Morientes

Cole

Boa Morte Radzinski

Pembridge Clark (c) Diop

Bocanegra Rehman Knight Rosenior

van der Sar

Hamann, Smicer, Warnock, Carson, Pellegrino

Goma, Crossley, Legwinski, Jensen, McBride

Liverpool heaped further pressure on their Merseyside rivals in the chase for Champions League football, defeating a spirited Fulham side 3-1 at Anfield.

A first goal at his new home from Fernando Morientes was soon cancelled out by Andrew Cole, before second-half efforts from Sami Hyypia and Milan Baros secured the three points for Rafael Benitez's team.

The men in red went in front after just nine minutes, as two Spaniards combined to deadly effect.

Luis Garcia sent over an inviting cross from the right, and Morientes lost his marker to angle a perfect header past a static Edwin van der Sar from 10 yards.

Home joy was short-lived, however, as Chris Coleman's side drew level seven minutes later.

STATISTICS

Season	Fixture	👕		🧤	Fixture	Season
172	7		Shots On Target		2	123
180	3		Shots Off Target		4	116
5	0		Hit Woodwork		0	3
63	1		Caught Offside		2	63
150	4		Corners		3	129
311	12		Fouls		13	323
54%	60%		Possession		40%	48%

Tomasz Radzinski is shadowed by Djimi Traore

Mark Pembridge holds off Steve Finnan

LEAGUE STANDINGS

Position (pos before)	W	D	L	F	A	Pts
5 (5) Liverpool	13	4	9	41	27	43
15 (15) Fulham	8	5	13	33	44	29

PREMIERSHIP MILESTONE

175 Andrew Cole scored his 175th Premiership goal.

PREMIERSHIP MILESTONE

150 Lee Clark made his 150th Premiership appearance on his 50th top-flight outing for Fulham.

> **"You can't afford to nod off and lose your men like we did three times against a good side like Liverpool."**
>
> Chris Coleman

Mark Pembridge won possession and fed Luis Boa Morte down the left, the former Arsenal winger then producing an accurate ball to the back post that a diving Cole headed beyond Jerzy Dudek.

After former Evertonian Tomasz Radzinski had sent a header narrowly wide, great skill from Morientes down the left eventually resulted in a venomous low drive from Igor Biscan that was well kept out by the Cottagers' giant Dutch keeper.

The game continued to be evenly contested after the interval. John Arne Riise linked up well with Baros on one occasion, while the pace of Boa Morte was a constant threat for the visitors.

Whichever team scored the next goal would have a great chance to win, and it was Liverpool who got it, Steven Gerrard's vicious inswinging free-kick from the left glanced home by an unmarked Hyypia in the 63rd minute.

Thereafter, the Reds assumed total control. Substitute Dietmar Hamann stung the palms of van der Sar, before Baros slammed the ball home from eight yards after Morientes had released Riise on the left.

The Czech striker was afforded a rapturous reception when he was replaced by his international colleague Vladimir Smicer five minutes later, the home fans fully appreciating the hard work he had put in for the cause.

Tottenham Hotspur 2
Fulham 0

Fixture Type: **Barclays Premiership** Date: **Saturday February 26 2005** Venue: **White Hart Lane**
Attendance: **35,885** Referee: **NS Barry**

PREMIERSHIP FIXTURE HISTORY

	Pl: 4	Draws: 1		Wins ⚽	☐	■
Tottenham Hotspur		2	7	4		1
Fulham		1	4	7		1

STARTING LINE-UPS

⚫ Kanoute, Keane, Cerny, Pamarot, Ziegler

⚪ John, McBride, Crossley, Volz, Legwinski

Substitute strikers Fredi Kanoute and Robbie Keane emerged from the bench to settle this London derby in Tottenham's favour.

Spurs came into the game on the back of a terrible recent record in capital clashes. The men from White Hart Lane had won just one of their previous 22 derby matches in the Premiership, and looked set to extend that hopeless record until late on.

Martin Jol opted to revert to the strike pairing of Mido and Jermain Defoe that had served him so well in the last League game against Portsmouth. Andy Reid also returned, having been cup-tied for the FA Cup clashes with West Brom and his old club Nottingham Forest.

Visiting boss Chris Coleman welcomed back Danish midfielder Claus Jensen to his top-flight starting XI for the first time since late October. Defender Alain Goma had been absent from Premiership action for slightly longer, and also returned.

Zat Knight keeps a close eye on Andy Reid

STATISTICS

Season	Fixture ⚫		⚪ Fixture	Season
166	8	Shots On Target	5	128
151	11	Shots Off Target	3	119
10	0	Hit Woodwork	0	3
105	6	Caught Offside	9	72
137	14	Corners	2	131
325	6	Fouls	13	336
50%	52%	Possession	48%	48%

Papa Bouba Diop bursts forward

It was the home side who began brightly, with Mido a constant threat. The Egyptian dragged a shot wide after just four minutes, and then fired over when picked out inside the box by Welsh midfielder Simon Davies.

The pressure continued apace, as Andrew Cole cleared Michael Brown's 22nd-minute effort off the line, before Edwin van der Sar plunged low to his right to turn away a long-range drive from the lively Reid. Captain Ledley King then saw a header deflected narrowly wide, as Tottenham failed to capitalise on their dominance.

Fulham's only attempt worthy of a mention was a powerful shot from distance by Papa Bouba Diop after 43 minutes. Unfortunately for the midfielder, the strike worried the crowd behind the goal more than it did Paul Robinson.

The second period was a carbon copy of the first, except that Jol's team eventually made a breakthrough. Having been on the field just five minutes, Kanoute curled a 25-yard free-kick from the inside-left channel around the wall and into the unguarded bottom-right corner.

The Frenchman then teed up Keane for an unbelievable close-range miss, before the Republic of Ireland international made amends in stoppage time as he outmuscled Luis Boa Morte and rounded van der Sar to tap home.

EVENT LINE		
HALF TIME 0 - 0		
59	⇄	Cole (Off) John (On)
73	⇄	**Defoe (Off) Kanoute (On)**
77	☐	Clark (Foul)
78	⚽	**Kanoute (Direct Free Kick)**
79	⇄	**Mido (Off) Keane (On)**
86	⇄	Jensen (Off) McBride (On)
90	⚽	**Keane (Open Play)**
FULL TIME 2 - 0		

LEAGUE STANDINGS						
Position (pos before)	W	D	L	F	A	Pts
8 (9) Tottenham H	11	6	10	35	30	39
15 (15) Fulham	8	5	14	33	46	29

"My two central defenders played really well, and you would expect our keeper to deal with the free-kick which Kanoute scored from."

Chris Coleman

Fulham 0
Charlton Athletic 0

Fixture Type: **Barclays Premiership** Date: **Saturday March 5 2005** Venue: **Craven Cottage**
Attendance: **18,290** Referee: **SG Bennett**

PREMIERSHIP FIXTURE HISTORY

	Pl: 4	Draws: 2	Wins ⚽	☐	■
Fulham		2	3	7	0
Charlton Athletic		0	0	6	0

STARTING LINE-UPS

🧤 John, Crossley, Volz, Legwinski, Radzinski

🧤 Johansson, Andersen, Fish, Euell, Jeffers

STATISTICS

Season	Fixture 🧤		🧤 Fixture	Season
133	5	Shots On Target	6	125
124	5	Shots Off Target	3	100
3	0	Hit Woodwork	1	6
74	2	Caught Offside	3	95
136	5	Corners	5	119
345	9	Fouls	12	355
48%	47%	Possession	53%	45%

Fulham moved a point closer to Premiership survival, thanks largely to some poor finishing from Charlton striker Shaun Bartlett.

Despite some unhappiness on the terraces, home boss Chris Coleman kept faith with his 4-5-1 formation. Alan Curbishley set out his team in the same fashion, and it was the visitors that began the game brightly.

Paul Konchesky did well on the left of the area and drove dangerously across the six-yard box. It seemed that Bartlett had arrived right on cue for a simple tap-in, but the South African somehow managed to get the ball stuck under his feet, before seeing a swivelling effort blocked.

Fulham defender Zat Knight then came close to opening the scoring twice in quick succession. The tall centre-back rose to head a left-wing corner narrowly wide at the back post, and then forced a plunging save from Dean Kiely as he unleashed a 30-yard drive.

Then came Bartlett's second notable miss, though this time Edwin van der Sar deserved a lot of credit. The Addicks broke down the right, with Matt Holland inadvertently finding his colleague on the left edge of the six-yard box. Again the South African swivelled and fired goalwards, only for the keeper to trap the ball between his right foot and the left-hand upright.

Alain Goma headed wide for the Cottagers, before Danny Murphy tested the keeper's reflexes from distance as the half drew to a close.

Unusually, the second period was less exciting than the first. A sprawling save from Kiely denied Goma, as Fulham's best chances continued to come from set-pieces.

Both Radostin Kishishev and Liam Rosenior resorted to trying their luck from distance, with drives that summed up how poor the game had become. Forwards Collins John and Jonatan Johansson were sent on, as the two managers looked to steal the points.

It was Charlton that came closest to doing just that, as van der Sar acrobatically repelled a Konchesky drive that was destined for the top-left corner.

Edwin van der Sar somehow keeps Charlton at bay

EVENT LINE

12	☐	**Boa Morte (Ung.Conduct)**
21	☐	Kishishev (Foul)
40	☐	**Goma (Foul)**
	HALF TIME 0 - 0	
60	☐	**Cole (Ung.Conduct)**
60	☐	El Karkouri (Foul)
73	⇄	**Jensen (Off) John (On)**
75	⇄	Thomas (Off) Johansson (On)
	FULL TIME 0 - 0	

LEAGUE STANDINGS

Position (pos before)	W	D	L	F	A	Pts
14 (15) Fulham	**8**	**6**	**14**	**33**	**46**	**30**
8 (9) Charlton Ath	11	7	10	32	38	40

"It has taken Charlton a long time to get to where they are, and it is not going to happen for us overnight."

Chris Coleman

Talal El Karkouri throws himself to the ground

Manchester United 1
Fulham 0

Fixture Type: **Barclays Premiership** Date: **Saturday March 19 2005** Venue: **Old Trafford**
Attendance: **67,959** Referee: **AP D'Urso**

PREMIERSHIP FIXTURE HISTORY

Pl: **4** Draws: **0**		Wins ⚽	▢	▪
Manchester United	3	8	6	0
Fulham	1	5	5	0

STARTING LINE-UPS

⚽ Smith, O'Shea, P Neville, Carroll, G Neville

⚽ Legwinski, Radzinski, Crossley, Volz, John

STATISTICS

Season	Fixture	⚽	⚽ Fixture	Season
245	12	Shots On Target	6	139
213	7	Shots Off Target	4	128
14	0	Hit Woodwork	1	4
114	2	Caught Offside	2	76
237	18	Corners	3	139
361	7	Fouls	11	356
55%	59%	Possession	41%	47%

Papa Bouba Diop protects the ball from Gabriel Heinze

Manchester United made hard work of beating Fulham, and were nearly made to pay for their wasteful finishing late on.

Sir Alex Ferguson's side dominated the opening period, as the visitors barely crossed the halfway line. Cristiano Ronaldo was at the heart of all his team's good work, and netted the only goal of the game after 21 minutes.

Receiving possession from Roy Keane on the left, the Portuguese winger cut inside Liam Rosenior and hammered a 20-yard effort into the top-right corner. The former Sporting Lisbon youngster had already headed narrowly wide, and was proving a constant menace to Chris Coleman's defence.

Prior to the goal, United had carved out a plethora of chances. Wayne Rooney missed the target with a flicked

Carlos Bocanegra keeps tabs on Wayne Rooney

> **"We were cautious in the first half, but went out in the second with more belief and had chances to equalise."**
>
> Chris Coleman

effort, Paul Scholes tried his luck with a header, and both Roy Keane and Gabriel Heinze went close from distance.

Having opened the scoring, Ronaldo then spurned a great opportunity to add a second when he failed to make proper contact with a 12-yard volley. A deflected Heinze strike then flew wide, as the home side went in at the interval with just a 1-0 lead.

The second 45 minutes began in a similar vein. Edwin van der Sar made two smart saves to keep out long-range Rooney attempts, while Ronaldo twice failed to hit the target. Two further stops from stinging Heinze drives kept the Cottagers in contention.

Having completely run the show for 80 minutes, the Old Trafford side appeared to run out of steam. A Beckham-esque clipped effort from halfway by Alan Smith was all that Ferguson's men could muster, as Fulham went close to an equaliser on three occasions.

Firstly, visiting captain Lee Clark saw his strike deflected against a post, with Carlos Bocanegra's follow-up somehow staying out. Then, Tim Howard deflected away the returning Andrew Cole's low drive, before late substitute Tomasz Radzinski failed to make decent contact with an inviting ball in from the right.

Fulham 3
Portsmouth 1

Fixture Type: **Barclays Premiership** Date: **Sunday April 3 2005** Venue: **Craven Cottage**
Attendance: **20,502** Referee: **M Clattenburg**

PREMIERSHIP FIXTURE HISTORY

Pl: **2**	Draws: **0**	Wins ⊙	☐	■
Fulham	2	5	3	0
Portsmouth	0	1	6	1

STARTING LINE-UPS

van der Sar

Volz Knight Goma Rosenior

Legwinski

Malbranque Jensen

Clark (c)
Boa Morte Cole

Yakubu LuaLua

Berger Stone
Cisse Skopelitis

Taylor Primus
Stefanovic De Zeeuw (c)

Ashdown

🧤 McBride,
Radzinski,
Bocanegra,
Crossley,

🧤 O'Neil, Kamara,
Fuller, Chalkias,
Hughes

Fulham produced a superb second-half performance to ease their relegation worries and drop Portsmouth back into the scrap at the bottom of the table.

The first chance fell to the visitors, Lomana LuaLua working his way down the left flank before drilling a dangerous ball across the face of goal for Steve Stone, who was just beaten to it by keeper Edwin van der Sar.

There was an opening for Patrik Berger soon after following some neat set-up play from LuaLua, but the Czech international's first touch let him down.

It took a stunning save from van der Sar to deny Portsmouth on 22 minutes, the Dutchman reacting brilliantly to turn LuaLua's point-blank header from Stone's cross over the bar.

Sylvain Legwinski then had a chance for Fulham, steering his header wide from a good position.

Zat Knight climbs highest

STATISTICS

Season	Fixture 🧤		🧤 Fixture	Season
146	7	Shots On Target	5	151
133	5	Shots Off Target	4	155
4	0	Hit Woodwork	0	6
78	2	Caught Offside	5	84
144	5	Corners	5	155
370	14	Fouls	10	375
48%	61%	Possession	39%	47%

Brian McBride celebrates with Steed Malbranque

EVENT LINE	
5	☐ Stefanovic (Foul)
32	⚽ Lua Lua (Open Play)
HALF TIME 0 - 1	
57	☐ **Rosenior (Handball)**
57	🔄 **Jensen (Off) McBride (On)**
63	⚽ **Cole (Open Play)**
64	🔄 **Legwinski (Off) Radzinski (On)**
77	🔄 Stone (Off) O'Neil (On)
79	☐ **Goma (Foul)**
80	☐ Skopelitis (Foul)
81	⚽ **McBride (Open Play)**
82	☐ **Boa Morte (Ung.Conduct)**
82	🔄 Berger (Off) Kamara (On)
83	☐ O'Neil (Foul)
84	🔄 **Clark (Off) Bocanegra (On)**
88	🔄 Yakubu (Off) Fuller (On)
90	⚽ **Boa Morte (Open Play)**
FULL TIME 3 - 1	

It seemed only a matter of time before Portsmouth scored the goal their dominating play deserved and on 32 minutes it duly arrived, LuaLua cutting back on the left side of the area and taking the ball past Zat Knight and Moritz Volz before curling a shot into the bottom corner from 18 yards.

The Cottagers wasted a prime opportunity to level matters on the stroke of half-time after Dejan Stefanovic handled Andrew Cole's cross into the Portsmouth area, Steed Malbranque's penalty saved by Jamie Ashdown diving to his left.

Fulham came out for the second period looking far more determined and were rewarded with a 63rd-minute equaliser, Luis Boa Morte advancing down the left before pulling the ball back for Cole to side-foot into the top corner.

Cole almost grabbed a second with 15 minutes to play, his sliding effort striking the inside of the post and rebounding back into play.

Aiyegbeni Yakubu then fired narrowly wide for Portsmouth before substitute Brian McBride moved Fulham ahead on 81 minutes, intercepting Arjan De Zeeuw's attempted header back to the keeper and sending a looping shot over Ashdown.

LuaLua responded with a dangerous ball into the box, but van der Sar made the grab.

Boa Morte sealed the win in the dying stages, robbing Linvoy Primus and rounding Ashdown before slotting home.

LEAGUE STANDINGS						
Position (pos before)	W	D	L	F	A	Pts
14 (16) Fulham	9	6	15	36	48	33
16 (15) Portsmouth	8	7	16	33	49	31

"Our second-half performance was magnificent. That's the sort of character you need when you're in the position we are."

Chris Coleman

Bolton Wanderers 3
Fulham 1

Fixture Type: **Barclays Premiership** Date: **Saturday April 9 2005** Venue: **Reebok Stadium**
Attendance: **25,493** Referee: **DJ Gallagher**

PREMIERSHIP FIXTURE HISTORY

	Pl: **4** Draws: **2**	Wins ⚽	▢	◼
Bolton Wanderers	1	3	3	0
Fulham	1	3	6	1

STARTING LINE-UPS

Jaaskelainen

Hunt   Ben Haim   N'Gotty   Candela

Okocha (c)   Hierro   Speed

Giannakopoulos   Nolan

Davies

McBride   Cole

Boa Morte   Malbranque

Clark (c)   Jensen

Rosenior   Volz

Goma   Knight

van der Sar

🧤 Gardner, Fadiga,
Poole, Jaidi,
Pedersen

👕 Radzinski, John,
Crossley,
Bocanegra,
Pembridge

Zat Knight surges away from Kevin Davies

STATISTICS

Season	Fixture	🧤		👕 Fixture	Season
201	11	Shots On Target	4	150
178	5	Shots Off Target	3	136
7	0	Hit Woodwork	0	4
88	7	Caught Offside	4	82
173	4	Corners	6	150
437	6	Fouls	14	384
49%	54%	Possession	46%	48%

Bolton Wanderers stayed on track for a possible European place with a convincing victory over 10-man Fulham.

Wanderers boss Sam Allardyce made one change to the side beaten at Liverpool the previous week, recalling captain Jay-Jay Okocha following the Nigerian's recovery from a knee injury.

Fulham boss Chris Coleman also made a change, opting to start Brian McBride up front alongside Andrew Cole.

The visitors were reduced to 10 men in the 12th minute after former Wanderer Claus Jensen used his arm to block a Bruno N'Gotty header which was destined for the back of the net. Okocha fired home the resulting penalty.

Brian McBride fends off Vincent Candela

Wanderers pressed for a second goal, Kevin Nolan and Gary Speed both wasting chances from good positions before Nolan beat Edwin van der Sar from close range on 33 minutes for his fourth of the season.

Fulham pulled one back on 47 minutes, Cole doing well to hold play up on the edge of the area before knocking a ball to the far post for Luis Boa Morte to slide home.

Fulham's joy was short-lived, however, as seven minutes later Stelios Giannakopoulos converted his sixth of the season to restore Bolton's two-goal advantage.

The hard-working Fulham midfield began to tire as the half progressed, opening extra space for Okocha and Stelios to attack van der Sar's goal.

Despite Wanderers' dominance, Fulham still managed to create a few good chances, McBride just missing out on Moritz Volz's ball from the right across the face of goal.

Coleman brought on Tomasz Radzinski and Collins John for Steed Malbranque and Cole for the final 10 minutes in the hope that fresh legs might catch out Wanderers.

Allardyce responded with two substitutions of his own, introducing Ricardo Gardner and Khalilou Fadiga for Vincent Candela and Fernando Hierro.

Okocha then wasted a chance for a Wanderers fourth, firing a free kick from a dangerous position straight into the defensive wall.

John looked to have grabbed a late goal for Fulham when he knocked the ball towards an empty net, only for Gardner to race back and clear off the line with an overhead kick.

LEAGUE STANDINGS

Position (pos before)	W	D	L	F	A	Pts
6 (6) Bolton W	14	7	11	41	36	49
16 (14) Fulham	9	6	16	37	51	33

> **"After the sending off it was always going to be an uphill struggle, but the boys never stopped working."**
>
> **Assistant Manager Steve Kean**

Fulham 1
Manchester City 1

Fixture Type: **Barclays Premiership** Date: **Saturday April 16 2005** Venue: **Craven Cottage**
Attendance: **21,796** Referee: **NS Barry**

PREMIERSHIP FIXTURE HISTORY

	Pl: 3 Draws: 2	Wins ●	□	■
Fulham	0	3	2	0
Manchester City	1	4	7	0

STARTING LINE-UPS

van der Sar
Volz   Knight   Goma   Rosenior
Malbranque   Clark (c)   Pembridge   Boa Morte
Cole   McBride
Fowler
Sibierski
Musampa   Reyna
Barton   Bosvelt
Jordan   Onuoha
Distin (c)   Dunne
James

⚽ Radzinski, John   ⚽ S Wright-Phillips
Crossley,   B Wright-Phillips
Bocanegra   Weaver, Thatcher
Rehman   Mills

STATISTICS

Season	Fixture ⚽		⚽ Fixture	Season
153	3	Shots On Target	3	177
141	5	Shots Off Target	4	169
5	1	Hit Woodwork	0	3
84	2	Caught Offside	11	105
156	6	Corners	8	205
393	9	Fouls	19	414
48%	45%	Possession	55%	49%

It was a return to the days of good old-fashioned centre-forward play at Craven Cottage, as Luis Boa Morte profited from a strong Brian McBride challenge to earn his side a point.

A suspiciously offside-looking Claudio Reyna – a one-time Fulham transfer target – had moved the visitors into a 20th-minute lead, before parity was restored 14 minutes from time.

Edwin van der Sar had already been forced to turn over a curling Antoine Sibierski effort, when he was called upon to deny the Frenchman for a second time. The Dutch custodian could only parry a diving header, enabling Reyna to steer home the loose ball from close range.

An angled Boa Morte drive was touched on to the base of the right-hand upright by David James, as the

Luis Boa Morte celebrates his goal

Brian McBride causes a problem for David James

EVENT LINE

20 ⚽ Reyna (Open Play)

HALF TIME 0 - 1

62 🔄 Fowler (Off) Wright-Phillips S (On)

66 🔄 **Malbranque (Off) Radzinski (On)**

69 🔄 **Cole (Off) John (On)**

76 ⚽ **Boa Morte (Open Play)**

81 🟨 Dunne (Foul)

86 🔄 Musampa (Off) Wright-Phillips B (On)

FULL TIME 1 - 1

LEAGUE STANDINGS

Position (pos before)	W	D	L	F	A	Pts
16 (16) Fulham	9	7	16	38	52	34
11 (11) Man City	10	11	12	39	37	41

"Results elsewhere went our way, so a point is not the end of the world."

Chris Coleman

Cottagers sought to find a way back into the match as half-time approached.

Home hopes should have been extinguished in the early stages of the second period. Sloppy play from several men in white shirts handed Robbie Fowler a decent sight of goal, but the former Liverpool striker drove the ball wide of the near post with his unfavoured right foot.

Stuart Pearce acted swiftly to replace his misfiring frontman with Shaun Wright-Phillips. The England international was making a welcome return from injury, and was soon followed on to the pitch by Tomasz Radzinski and Collins John.

It was John who almost made an immediate impact, firing in a deflected 20-yard effort that looped just the wrong side of the right-hand upright. A Fulham goal was not long in coming, however, as Boa Morte struck in the 76th minute.

Lee Clark hoisted over a deep cross from the right that McBride challenged for with the keeper. The ball broke loose as the two players collided, with the US international having the presence of mind to tee up Boa Morte for a crisp 13-yard finish through a sea of bodies.

The visiting players felt that James had been fouled, but referee Neale Barry waved away their protests.

There was still time for both teams to go close, through Kiki Musampa and Radzinski, but a draw was probably a fair result.

Middlesbrough 1
Fulham 1

Fixture Type: **Barclays Premiership** Date: **Tuesday April 19 2005** Venue: **Riverside Stadium**
Attendance: **30,650** Referee: **R Styles**

PREMIERSHIP FIXTURE HISTORY

Pl: 4	Draws: 2	Wins ⚽	☐	■
Middlesbrough		2	7	7	0
Fulham		0	5	6	0

STARTING LINE-UPS

🎽 Kennedy, Knight   🎽 Malbranque,
Davies, Wheater   Crossley,
Doriva   Bocanegra,
                       Rehman

STATISTICS

Season	Fixture 🎽		🎽 Fixture	Season
227	5	Shots On Target	2	155
173	3	Shots Off Target	5	146
6	0	Hit Woodwork	1	6
90	5	Caught Offside	3	87
183	2	Corners	6	162
413	11	Fouls	12	405
50%	52%	Possession	48%	48%

Mark Pembridge helps the ball on

A poor game sprang into life in the final 10 minutes, with Brian McBride's goal cancelled out by a highly controversial last-gasp penalty.

With more points required to ensure their Premiership survival, Fulham looked hungrier than their UEFA Cup-chasing opponents. An early free-kick nearly led to a goal, McBride directing a six-yard header just the wrong side of the left-hand upright.

Edwin van der Sar was a virtual spectator during the opening period, and looked on as Jimmy Floyd Hasselbaink tumbled in the box. Referee Rob Styles justifiably waved away his appeals, though the striker was not happy.

Despite being clearly offside, a McBride header that flew over would have counted. That effort followed a wayward finish from Collins John, the young striker blazing over from a central position inside the area.

The Cottagers remained on top after the interval, and

Brian McBride celebrates opening the scoring

LEAGUE STANDINGS

Position (pos before)	W	D	L	F	A	Pts
8 (8) Middlesbrough	12	10	11	46	44	46
15 (16) Fulham	9	8	16	39	53	35

PREMIERSHIP MILESTONE

150 Luis Boa Morte made his 150th Premiership appearance.

PREMIERSHIP MILESTONE

50 Brian McBride made his 50th Premiership appearance.

"It was disappointing to say the least. We should be going home with three points."

Chris Coleman on dubious late penalty

were desperately unlucky not to take the lead from a Luis Boa Morte free-kick. Stand-in Boro keeper Brad Jones was left rooted to the spot, as the Portugal international's curling effort struck the top of his crossbar.

Just 13 minutes remained when Boro carved out their first genuine chance of the contest. Boudewijn Zenden whipped in a near-post delivery from the left, and Hasselbaink got away from his marker to glance a header dangerously across the face of goal.

Five minutes later Fulham went in front. Tomasz Radzinski was allowed to make progress down the right, with McBride on hand to sweep his low cross back from the direction it came and just inside the far upright from 15 yards.

Given the way in which their team had performed, the Riverside faithful had little reason to expect a reply. They got one, however, as the referee handed them a late lifeline.

Van der Sar charged from his goal in an attempt to clear the ball from danger, but succeeded only in upending Hasselbaink. Despite the foul taking place a good yard outside the area, Styles awarded a penalty that Zenden converted with ease.

Chelsea 3
Fulham 1

Fixture Type: **Barclays Premiership** Date: **Saturday April 23 2005** Venue: **Stamford Bridge**
Attendance: **42,081** Referee: **A Wiley**

PREMIERSHIP FIXTURE HISTORY

Pl: **4**	Draws: **1**	Wins ⚽	☐	◼
Chelsea	3	9	6	0
Fulham	0	5	5	0

STARTING LINE-UPS

Cech
Johnson Carvalho Terry (c) Huth
Gudjohnsen Makelele Lampard
J Cole Duff
Drogba

McBride John
Boa Morte Radzinski
Pembridge Clark (c)
Rosenior Volz
Goma Knight
van der Sar

👕 Jarosik, Robben, Tiago, Cudicini, Kezman 👕 Malbranque, Crossley, Bocanegra, Rehman, Jensen

STATISTICS

Season	Fixture 👕		👕 Fixture	Season
263	7	Shots On Target	4	159
223	5	Shots Off Target	6	152
10	0	Hit Woodwork	0	6
114	11	Caught Offside	1	88
226	4	Corners	6	168
421	7	Fouls	11	416
56%	52%	Possession	48%	48%

Chelsea moved to within touching distance of their first League title in 50 years, defeating neighbours Fulham 3-1 at Stamford Bridge.

Joe Cole's 17th-minute opener was cancelled out by Collins John four minutes before the break, with second-half strikes from Frank Lampard and Eidur Gudjohnsen ensuring that the Premiership trophy would be heading to West London if nearest challengers Arsenal failed to beat Tottenham two days later.

With a Champions League semi-final meeting with Liverpool on the horizon, José Mourinho would have been hoping for a comfortable afternoon. That looked a possibility when Cole was allowed to turn on the edge of the box and curl an effort just inside the right-hand post.

Moritz Volz tussles with Eidur Gudjohnsen

Collins John brushes aside Ricardo Carvalho

Chelsea then enjoyed a decent spell. Didier Drogba, who had earlier headed narrowly over from a Damien Duff cross, went close to making it two when he spun and quickly sent an effort just past the left-hand upright.

The Cottagers weathered the storm, however, and began to create chances of their own as the half progressed. Brian McBride fired over after good work from Liam Rosenior down the left, before John made it 1-1 on 41 minutes.

The powerful young forward seemed second favourite to reach Luis Boa Morte's ball behind the defence, but he got the better of Ricardo Carvalho to slot past Petr Cech from just inside the six-yard box.

Arjen Robben was introduced at the start of the second period, returning to action following a month on the sidelines.

The Dutchman made an immediate impact, setting up Gudjohnsen for a disallowed goal before teeing up Lampard for a strike that did count.

The England international arrived in customary fashion in the 64th minute, placing a 15-yard effort low to the right of a wrong-footed Edwin van der Sar.

Tomasz Radzinski showed that Fulham were still a threat with a shot from distance that called Cech into action, but Gudjohnsen sealed the points with three minutes remaining as he raced on to Tiago's pass and slotted the ball under the keeper.

EVENT LINE

17	⚽ Cole J (Open Play)
41	⚽ John (Open Play)
43	▢ Terry (Foul)
HALF TIME 1 - 1	
46	⮀ Cole J (Off) Robben (On)
46	⮀ Huth (Off) Jarosik (On)
53	▢ John (Handball)
64	⚽ Lampard (Open Play)
74	⮀ Drogba (Off) Tiago (On)
84	⮀ Pembridge (Off) Malbranque (On)
87	⚽ Gudjohnsen (Open Play)
FULL TIME 3 - 1	

LEAGUE STANDINGS

Position (pos before)	W	D	L	F	A	Pts
1 (1) Chelsea	26	7	1	65	13	85
16 (15) Fulham	9	8	17	40	56	35

"I thought our guys played very well. I think we pushed them from the first to the last minute."

Chris Coleman

Fulham 2
Everton 0

Fixture Type: **Barclays Premiership** Date: **Saturday April 30 2005** Venue: **Craven Cottage**
Attendance: **21,881** Referee: **SG Bennett**

PREMIERSHIP FIXTURE HISTORY

Pl: 4 Draws: 0		Wins ⚽	☐	◼
Fulham	4	8	4	2
Everton	0	1	7	1

STARTING LINE-UPS

van der Sar

Volz — Knight — Goma — Rosenior

Clark (c) — Diop — Boa Morte
Radzinski

McBride — John

Ferguson — Bent

Kilbane — Arteta — Carsley — Cahill

Pistone — Weir (c) — Yobo — Watson

Martyn

🧤 Cole, Jensen, Crossley, Bocanegra, Pembridge

👕 Osman, McFadden, Beattie, Wright, Plessis

STATISTICS

Season	Fixture	🏴		👕	Fixture	Season
165	6		Shots On Target	4		165
157	5		Shots Off Target	7		186
6	0		Hit Woodwork	0		6
90	2		Caught Offside	9		91
171	3		Corners	7		172
434	18		Fouls	16		434
48%	52%		Possession	48%		49%

First-half goals from Collins John and Brian McBride saw off the challenge of Everton, and confirmed that Fulham would be playing Premiership football again next season.

David Moyes's men almost got off to a dream start when Kevin Kilbane thought he had opened the scoring. The Republic of Ireland international was correctly ruled offside, however, as he touched home David Weir's header from a free-kick.

Star midfielder Tim Cahill limped off in the 13th minute, with the Cottagers taking the lead shortly afterwards.

Former Toffee Tomasz Radzinski saw his shot charged down, but John reacted quickly to lash the ball home from near the penalty spot.

The game was very open, with both sides continuing to create chances.

Goalscorer John dragged a low effort past the left-hand upright, before Marcus Bent whipped in a dangerous angled drive from the right side of the area at the other end.

The next goal was going to prove vital, and it went to Chris Coleman's team.

Luis Boa Morte seemed to take an eternity before delivering from the left, but his patience was rewarded as McBride rose to plant a towering 14-yard header beyond the reach of Nigel Martyn after 39 minutes.

Edwin van der Sar foiled a clearly offside Bent with his legs shortly before the break, while Lee Carsley shanked a 12-yard volley wide from an unmarked position during the early stages of the second period.

Papa Bouba Diop was booked for a lunging challenge on Leon Osman after 68 minutes, and was then harshly shown a second yellow card by referee Steve Bennett for minimal contact with Everton substitute James McFadden.

Another replacement, James Beattie, went close with a free-kick in the final minute, but 10-man Fulham held on to record an important victory.

Collins John enjoys his moment of glory

LEAGUE STANDINGS

Position (pos before)	W	D	L	F	A	Pts
15 (16) Fulham	**10**	**8**	**17**	**42**	**56**	**38**
4 (4) Everton	17	7	11	41	36	58

"This season we have been too inconsistent, and today we showed exactly what we are capable of."

Chris Coleman

Lee Clark congratulates goalscorer Brian McBride

Fulham 1
Newcastle United 3

Fixture Type: **Barclays Premiership**   Date: **Wednesday May 4 2005**   Venue: **Craven Cottage**
Attendance: **19,003**   Referee: **G Poll**

PREMIERSHIP FIXTURE HISTORY

Pl: 4 Draws: 0		Wins ⚽	⬜	⬛
Fulham	2	8	4	0
Newcastle United	2	8	9	1

STARTING LINE-UPS

van der Sar

Volz   Knight   Goma   Rosenior

Pembridge

Radzinski   Boa Morte

Clark (c)

Cole   McBride

Kluivert

Ameobi   Milner

N'Zogbia   Faye   Ambrose

Taylor   Boumsong (c)   Bramble   Carr

Given

Jensen, Crossley, Bocanegra, Pearce, Rehman

O'Brien, Harper, Ramage, Brittain, Robert

Liam Rosenior surges past James Milner

STATISTICS

Season	Fixture	🅰	🅱	Fixture	Season
168	3	Shots On Target	3		249
160	3	Shots Off Target	1		213
6	0	Hit Woodwork	0		11
97	7	Caught Offside	6		96
172	1	Corners	2		230
445	11	Fouls	13		463
48%	62%	Possession	38%		50%

Newcastle rediscovered that winning feeling, picking up three points for the first time since early March.

Darren Ambrose, Patrick Kluivert and Shola Ameobi were on target for the Magpies, with former Everton man Tomasz Radzinski netting what proved to be nothing more than a late consolation for the home side.

The major team news centred around the non-appearance of Alan Shearer. The striker hadn't registered a Premiership goal in three months, and asked manager Graeme Souness if he could be rested for this trip to West London.

The absence of their captain didn't seem to affect United, as they made the better start. A right-wing cross was turned into the side-netting by Kluivert, while

Tomasz Radzinski outwits Jean-Alain Boumsong

EVENT LINE	
18 ⚽ Ambrose (Open Play)	
HALF TIME 0 - 1	
62 ⚽ Kluivert (Corner)	
62 🟨 **van der Sar (Dissent)**	
66 🔄 **Cole (Off) Jensen (On)**	
67 🟨 Taylor (Foul)	
75 ⚽ Ameobi (Corner)	
86 ⚽ **Radzinski (Open Play)**	
FULL TIME 1 - 3	

LEAGUE STANDINGS						
Position (pos before)	W	D	L	F	A	Pts
16 (15) Fulham	10	8	18	43	59	38
12 (14) Newcastle Utd	10	13	13	46	54	43

"I'm very disappointed tonight, particularly after the way we played on Saturday."

Chris Coleman

a neat move ended with the sting being taken out of an Ambrose drive.

The former Ipswich midfielder didn't have long to wait for a goal, however, steering the ball home from nine yards out after James Milner's deflected far-post header had fallen into his path.

All of Fulham's chances during the opening 45 minutes fell to former Magpies, centre-back Alain Goma missing with an early header before Lee Clark nodded just over following Shay Given's challenge on Andrew Cole.

Dutchman Kluivert had been guilty of a poor aerial miss in the first half, but he made amends just past the hour mark.

Charles N'Zogbia delivered a vicious inswinging corner from the right, and the former Barcelona man arrived to power home a near-post header.

Luis Boa Morte responded for the Cottagers, fizzing a 15-yard effort narrowly wide of the left-hand upright.

Any hopes of a home comeback were put to bed after 75 minutes, however, as Ameobi made it three. This time Chris Coleman's men failed to defend a corner from the opposite flank, with the striker rising virtually unopposed at the far post to convert Milner's delivery.

The Craven Cottage faithful were at least given an 86th-minute goal to cheer, Radzinski collecting from Liam Rosenior before tucking the ball under Given and into the far-right corner of the net.

Blackburn Rovers 1
Fulham 3

Fixture Type: **Barclays Premiership** Date: **Saturday May 7 2005** Venue: **Ewood Park**
Attendance: **18,991** Referee: **P Dowd**

PREMIERSHIP FIXTURE HISTORY

Pl: 4	Draws: 0		Wins ⚽	◻	◼
Blackburn Rovers		2	6	8	1
Fulham		2	6	8	1

STARTING LINE-UPS

Friedel

Short (c)   Nelson
Neill   Johansson
         Mokoena
     Reid   Savage
Emerton   Stead   Pedersen

McBride
        Malbranque
Boa Morte   Radzinski
    Pembridge   Clark (c)

Rosenior   Volz
      Goma   Knight

van der Sar

Thompson, Tugay, Derbyshire, Taylor, Enckelman

Bocanegra, Crossley, Pearce, Rehman, Timlin

Fulham produced a vintage display at Ewood Park, becoming the first team to net three goals against Blackburn in a Premiership match since late November.

Mark Hughes's team got off to a dream start, as Lucas Neill opened the scoring after just six minutes. The goal had an Australian flavour to it, the full-back surging on to Brett Emerton's pass before beating Edwin van der Sar from 12 yards.

That was as good as it got for Rovers, however, with the Cottagers drawing level midway through the half.

Captain Lee Clark ran on to a Moritz Volz chip and intelligently pulled the ball back from the right, where Steed Malbranque was waiting to slot home.

Things might have been different had Jonathan Stead's

STATISTICS

Season	Fixture ⚽		⚽ Fixture	Season
185	5	Shots On Target	7	175
227	8	Shots Off Target	1	161
8	1	Hit Woodwork	0	6
151	8	Caught Offside	0	97
207	8	Corners	5	177
591	12	Fouls	23	468
49%	54%	Possession	46%	48%

Brian McBride is mobbed after steering Fulham in front

Steed Malbranque makes it 3-1

> **"I was pleased with the effort of the team. We showed great character and a lot of composure on the ball."**
>
> **Chris Coleman**

left-footed curler not drifted just the wrong side of van der Sar's right-hand upright, but Fulham capitalised on their reprieve.

Zat Knight saw an early second-half header ruled out for climbing on a defender at a corner, before Brian McBride netted after 53 minutes.

A flag-kick from the right was flicked on by Clark, with the US international controlling and then sweeping the ball home from seven yards out at the far post.

An unmarked Emerton should have done better than strike the outside of a post, while Robbie Savage saw a penalty saved after Luis Boa Morte had hauled down Morten Gamst Pedersen at a free-kick.

It was after this that the fireworks really began. A crude Boa Morte challenge on Ryan Nelson provoked an angry reaction from Craig Short, with the stand-in Blackburn skipper receiving a red card for raising his hands.

Then, just a minute later, a rush of blood saw Liam Rosenior shove Savage to the ground. The defender clearly didn't like the former Leicester midfielder's strong challenge on his Portuguese team-mate, but left referee Phil Dowd with little option but to dismiss him.

With both teams down to 10 men, Fulham took advantage of the space on offer. An away victory was duly confirmed, as Malbranque rounded off a sweeping move by beating Brad Friedel with the outside of his right boot.

Fulham 6
Norwich City 0

Fixture Type: **Barclays Premiership** Date: **Sunday May 15 2005** Venue: **Craven Cottage**
Attendance: **21,927** Referee: **S Dunn**

PREMIERSHIP FIXTURE HISTORY

Pl: 1	Draws: 0		Wins ⚽	☐	◼
Fulham		1	6	0	0
Norwich City		0	0	1	0

STARTING LINE-UPS

van der Sar

Volz Knight Goma Bocanegra

Diop

Malbranque Boa Morte

Clark (c)

Radzinski McBride

McKenzie Ashton

Huckerby Bentley

Safri Francis

Drury Helveg

Shackell Fleming (c)

Green

Cole, Crossley, Pearce, Rehman, Pembridge

Holt, Jonson, Svensson, Ward, Charlton

Zat Knight is too strong for Dean Ashton

STATISTICS

Season	Fixture		Fixture	Season
184	9	Shots On Target	0	178
165	4	Shots Off Target	2	187
7	1	Hit Woodwork	0	6
98	1	Caught Offside	5	127
181	4	Corners	13	188
479	11	Fouls	12	520
48%	56%	Possession	44%	45%

Having battled hard to gain control of their Premiership destiny in recent weeks, Norwich exited the top-flight with something of a whimper.

The Canaries came into the game knowing that a first away win of the season would ensure survival, but suffered a humiliating six-goal drubbing that saw them return to the Championship at the first time of asking.

Nigel Worthington's men actually made an impressive start. Darren Huckerby's low drive was deflected wide, while the Cottagers were forced into several last-ditch challenges.

The visitors were dealt a hammer blow after just 10 minutes, however, as Brian McBride opened the scoring.

Tomasz Radzinski created the chance, slipping a ball into the inside-right channel that his team-mate poked under Robert Green.

Brian McBride enjoys his afternoon in the sun

"It was great to go out with a result like that, but of course I feel sorry for Nigel Worthington."

Chris Coleman

Dean Ashton was then harshly penalised for a foul as he rifled in what he thought was an equaliser, before Papa Bouba Diop stunned the travelling fans by netting an exquisite 25-yard free-kick in the 35th minute.

A stretching McBride hit the bar as half-time approached, and a third goal did arrive within 10 minutes of the restart. Defender Zat Knight was the unlikely scorer, lashing a 15-yard drive through a crowd of bodies at a corner.

The Canaries were now completely reliant on other results going their way, and went 4-0 down with 18 minutes remaining. Luis Boa Morte was given time and space in the box, eventually picking out Steed Malbranque for a cool 12-yard finish.

As Delia Smith watched on with her fellow supporters, McBride made it five. The American was released in the inside-left channel by Malbranque, and drove the ball comfortably past Green and into the far corner.

Andrew Cole, who had scored the winner in the reverse fixture, then emerged from the bench to add a cheeky sixth, the former England international deftly flicking home McBride's low cross to cap a miserable day for Norwich.

With only the result at St Mary's going in their favour, Worthington's team ended the day in 19th place. This defeat highlighted the two main reasons for their relegation – poor away form and a leaky defence.

Watford 1
Fulham 1

Fixture Type: **FA Cup Third Round** Date: **Saturday January 8 2005** Venue: **Vicarage Road**
Attendance: **14,896** Referee: **AP D'Urso**

FA CUP FIXTURE HISTORY

Pl: 3	Draws: 3	Wins ☺
Watford	0	3
Fulham	0	3

STARTING LINE-UPS

Chamberlain
Chambers · Cox (c) · Demerit · Darlington
Ardley
Gunnarsson · Mahon
Devlin · Bouazza
Helguson

Cole (c)
Boa Morte · John
Pembridge · Legwinski
Malbranque
Bocanegra · Fontaine · Knight · Rosenior
van der Sar

Blizzard, Doyley, McNamee , Dyer, Webber

Crossley, Rehman, Volz , Clark, McBride

STATISTICS

Fixture 🦌		Fixture 🏠
9	Shots On Target	6
9	Shots Off Target	5
0	Hit Woodwork	3
5	Caught Offside	4
3	Corners	3
7	Fouls	19

Fulham and Watford produced an entertaining Cup tie at Vicarage Road, with the 1-1 draw reflecting the even nature of the game.

Though the home side created a greater number of chances, Chris Coleman's men hit the woodwork on three separate occasions. Collins John was the first player to do so, striking the far post with a venomous cross-cum-shot.

Iceland international Heidar Helguson prodded a great opportunity narrowly wide, before the visitors took a 17th-minute lead. The giant figure of Zat Knight rose to meet a deep Mark Pembridge free-kick inside the six-yard box, as veteran keeper Alec Chamberlain failed to claim the delivery.

Having spurned several half-chances to draw level, Ray Lewington's charges conjured up a 42nd-minute equaliser. A goalmouth scramble ended with Hameur Bouazza being

Steed Malbranque is challenged by Brynjar Gunnarsson

Steed Malbranque surges past Gavin Mahon

FA CUP MILESTONE

Both Liam Rosenior and Andrew Cole made their first FA Cup appearances for Fulham.

FA CUP MILESTONE

Both Liam Fontaine and Collins John made their first FA Cup appearances.

FA CUP MILESTONE

Zat Knight netted his first senior goal.

"It was a good game. There were chances at both ends, and we knew it was never going to be easy."

Chris Coleman

upended, and Helguson coolly rolled the ball past Edwin van der Sar from the resulting penalty.

The second period was no less action-packed, with the Premiership outfit beginning in the ascendancy. Andrew Cole was denied by a post, while Steed Malbranque was unlucky to see his powerful drive rattle the crossbar shortly afterwards.

With the scalps of top-flight duo Southampton and Portsmouth under their belts in the Carling Cup, Watford weren't phased by the increased tempo of Fulham's football. The Hornets withstood everything that was thrown at them, and hit back as the game progressed.

The visiting defenders continued to struggle against the imposing physical presence of Helguson, and the tall striker should really have hit the target when rising to meet a deep delivery from the right wing.

Dutch custodian van der Sar was certainly made to earn his money on several other occasions, though, Gavin Mahon, Anthony McNamee and Bouazza all forcing the keeper into showing why he has so many international caps to his name.

Defeat would have been harsh on either side, with a replay suiting both parties. The Cottagers knew that they had every chance to make progress, while Watford could look forward to the extra revenue they would gain from a trip to Craven Cottage.

Fulham 2
Watford 0

Fixture Type: **FA Cup Third Round Replay** Date: **Wednesday January 19 2005** Venue: **Craven Cottage**
Attendance: **11,306** Referee: **AP D'Urso**

FA CUP FIXTURE HISTORY

Pl: **3** Draws: **0**		Wins ☺
Fulham	1	3
Watford	2	5

STARTING LINE-UPS

van der Sar

Volz Knight Rehman Bocanegra

Diop Clark (c) Legwinski

Radzinski Boa Morte

Cole

Helguson Webber

Bouazza Devlin

Mahon Blizzard

Darlington Chambers

Demerit Cox (c)

Chamberlain

⚽ Crossley, Rosenior, Pembridge, John, McBride

👕 Ardley, Doyley, Gunnarsson, Young, Dyer

STATISTICS

Fixture ⚽		Fixture 👕
4	Shots On Target	4
5	Shots Off Target	5
0	Hit Woodwork	0
6	Caught Offside	4
3	Corners	6
18	Fouls	10

Papa Bouba Diop in action

Goals from Moritz Volz and Tomasz Radzinski earned Fulham a comfortable 2-0 win against Watford in their F.A.Cup 3rd Round replay.

With a trip to Derby County awaiting the winners, both teams must have felt that they had a genuine chance to make progress in the competition. That was certainly evident in the early exchanges, as decent chances went begging at either end.

It didn't take long for Chris Coleman's side to get their noses in front, with Volz netting his first goal for the Club.

The German full-back rounded off a sweeping move with an unerring finish, latching on to Papa Bouba Diop's pass in the inside-right channel and driving the ball low across Alec Chamberlain.

Carlos Bocanegra closes down Danny Webber

EVENT LINE

13	⚽	**Volz (Open Play)**
	HALF TIME 1 - 0	
63	🔁	**Clark (Off) Pembridge (On)**
65	⚽	**Radzinski (Open Play)**
67	🔁	Blizzard (Off) Dyer (On)
67	🔁	Bouazza (Off) Ardley (On)
67	🔁	Devlin (Off) Gunnarsson (On)
71	🔁	**Cole (Off) McBride (On)**
84	🔁	**Boa Morte (Off) John (On)**
88	▢	**Rehman (Foul)**
89	▢	**Diop (Ung.Conduct)**
	FULL TIME 2 - 0	

FA CUP MILESTONE

Both Zesh Rehman and Papa Bouba Diop made their first F.A.Cup appearances.

FA CUP MILESTONE

Tomasz Radzinski marked his first FA Cup appearance for Fulham with a goal.

FA CUP MILESTONE

Moritz Volz netted his first goal for Fulham.

"**I worked the defence harder yesterday than I normally would do in a pre-match training session, and they put what I showed them into practice.**"

Chris Coleman

The strike seemed to knock the stuffing out of Ray Lewington's men, though they didn't succumb to a wave of home pressure. In fact, Danny Webber almost drew the Hornets level with a fine solo run that ended with a smothering save.

Portugal international Luis Boa Morte went closest to making it 2-0 in what remained of the first half. The former Arsenal and Southampton winger tried his luck with a free-kick, but curled the effort just inches the wrong side of an upright.

With four Carling Cup goals to his name, former Everton forward Radzinski had already demonstrated an ability to find the net in knockout competition. That trend continued in the 65th minute, as he ran on to Andrew Cole's pass and slotted the ball beyond the keeper.

There was no way back for the men from the Championship, though the introduction of Brynjar Gunnarsson, Neal Ardley and Bruce Dyer did bring renewed sparkle to their play in the closing stages of an encounter that had been contested in the right spirit.

Fulham did enough over the two ties to warrant making progress, though Watford didn't make life easy for their Premiership opponents. Heidar Helguson was a constant source of danger, and Edwin van der Sar was far more than an interested spectator in both matches.

The FA ⚊ CUP

Derby County 1
Fulham 1

Fixture Type: FA Cup Fourth Round **Date:** Saturday January 29 2005 **Venue:** Pride Park
Attendance: 22,040 Referee: **G Poll**

FA CUP FIXTURE HISTORY

Pl: **1** Draws: **1**	Wins ⚽	
Derby County	0	1
Fulham	0	1

STARTING LINE-UPS

Grant, Boertien, Bolder, Junior, Tudgay

Crossley, Pearce, Jensen, John, McBride

Luis Boa Morte pressurises Inigo Idiakez

STATISTICS

Fixture 🐏		Fixture 👤
3	Shots On Target	2
10	Shots Off Target	3
0	Hit Woodwork	0
1	Caught Offside	5
5	Corners	4
8	Fouls	12

For the second consecutive round, Fulham drew 1-1 at the ground of a Championship opponent.

An upset appeared on the cards when Marcus Tudgay steered Derby into a 56th-minute lead, but Collins John emerged from the bench to net an equaliser 19 minutes from time.

The first half wasn't particularly entertaining. George Burley's men probably shaded play, though they seldom threatened Edwin van der Sar's goal. Polish striker Grzegorz Rasiak was just unable to connect with a Marco Reich cross, while Tommy Smith saw a well-struck shot blocked by a defender.

In fact, the only genuine opportunity of the first 45 minutes fell to the visitors, Sylvain Legwinski missing the target under pressure from Tom Huddlestone.

Lee Clark closes in on Tom Huddlestone

Things opened up after the break, with substitute Tudgay quickly introducing himself to the action with a wayward header. Mark Pembridge then went close with a low shot, before the Derby replacement was more accurate with his second attempt.

Great work from Smith down the right ended with the ball being delivered towards the near post. While defenders stood like statues, Tudgay read the script to steal in and find the net from within the six-yard box.

With a disappointing exit staring them in the face, Chris Coleman's men responded in positive fashion. The Cottagers established territorial dominance, and then hit their hosts with a sucker punch.

Having entered the fray less than a minute earlier, John profited from confusion at the back to direct an eight-yard effort beyond Lee Camp. The striker was booked by referee Graham Poll for his over-exuberant celebrations, but he was too happy to care.

Fulham looked the more likely winners from this point on, though they survived a real scare late in the day. A diagonal pass found the lively Tudgay, and van der Sar had to be alert to repel his low shot.

EVENT LINE

HALF TIME 0 - 0	
46	**Reich (Off) Tudgay (On)**
56	**Tudgay (Open Play)**
70	Radzinski (Off) John (On)
71	John (Open Play)
72	John (Ung.Conduct)
80	**Idiakez (Dissent)**
80	Cole (Foul)
FULL TIME 1 - 1	

FA CUP MILESTONE

Collins John scored his first F.A.Cup goal.

> **"Derby are a very good team, but we have got them back to Craven Cottage and hopefully we can finish the job there."**
> **Chris Coleman**

Fulham 4
Derby County 2

Fixture Type: **FA Cup Fourth Round Replay** **Date:** **Saturday February 12 2005** **Venue:** **Craven Cottage**
Attendance: **15,528** **Referee:** **P Walton**

FA CUP FIXTURE HISTORY

Pl: 2 Draws: 0		Wins ⚽
Fulham	2	7
Derby County	0	2

STARTING LINE-UPS

Crossley, Goma, Jensen , John, McBride

Grant, Turner, Doyle, Junior, Peschisolido

STATISTICS

Fixture 🧤		Fixture 👕
9	Shots On Target	14
5	Shots Off Target	7
0	Hit Woodwork	0
3	Caught Offside	0
1	Corners	10
13	Fouls	8

Andrew Cole gets a toe to the ball

Fulham and Derby served up a six-goal thriller at Craven Cottage, with the Premiership side advancing after extra time.

As in the original tie at Pride Park, it was the Championship side that went in front. Just four minutes had elapsed when Grzegorz Rasiak turned home Tommy Smith's cross from the right, leaving the Cottagers shell-shocked.

The visitors had several chances to add a second goal. Inigo Idiakez was denied following impressive play from Morten Bisgaard, and the Dane nearly scored himself moments later with a shot from distance that troubled Edwin van der Sar.

Clause Jensen makes sure of progression

EVENT LINE

4	⚽ Rasiak (Indirect Free Kick)
28	🔄 Smith (Off) Junior (On)
45	⚽ **Diop (Penalty)**
	HALF TIME 1 - 1
46	🔄 **Rehman (Off) Goma (On)**
50	⚽ **Boa Morte (Open Play)**
57	▢ **Bocanegra (Foul)**
80	🔄 **Cole (Off) John (On)**
83	🔄 Bolder (Off) Peschisolido (On)
86	⚽ Peschisolido (Indirect Free Kick)
90	🔄 Junior (Off) Doyle (On)
94	⚽ **John (Indirect Free Kick)**
102	🔄 **Legwinski (Off) Jensen (On)**
105	⚽ **Jensen (Open Play)**
105	▢ Doyle (Foul)
	FULL TIME 4 - 2

Defender Zesh Rehman nearly scored a memorable own goal before Chris Coleman's charges at last awoke from a prolonged state of slumber, Tomasz Radzinski meeting Luis Boa Morte's 34th-minute cross on the volley, but sending the ball high over the bar.

The half ended as it had begun, with the Rams on top, though there was to be a twist in the tail.

A marauding Bisgaard curled an effort just past the post and Rasiak saw a header cleared off the line, with referee Peter Walton then awarding Fulham an injury-time penalty.

Michael Johnson was penalised for using his hand while making a sliding challenge, enabling Papa Bouba Diop to draw the sides level from the spot.

Things worsened for George Burley's men five minutes after the interval, as Boa Morte made it 2-1 with a low, right-footed shot.

Several good opportunities came and went for Derby before substitute Paul Peschisolido scrambled home a well-deserved equaliser four minutes from time.

The momentum appeared to have swung in favour of the visitors as the match moved into extra time, but it was Collins John who would find the back of the net, the young striker converting a swivelling left-footed effort from 12 yards.

Claus Jensen then became the third replacement to get his name on the scoresheet, sweeping a Radzinski pass beyond a helpless Lee Camp in the 105th minute.

FA CUP MILESTONE

Claus Jensen marked his first F.A.Cup appearance for Fulham with his first goal in the competition.

FA CUP MILESTONE

Papa Bouba Diop netted his first F.A.Cup goal.

> **"I think our lads showed a lot of bottle to bounce back from a poor first-half performance and eventually get through."**
>
> **Chris Coleman**

Bolton Wanderers 1
Fulham 0

Fixture Type: FA Cup Fifth Round Date: **Saturday February 19 2005** Venue: **Reebok Stadium**
Attendance: **16,151** Referee: **HM Webb**

FA CUP FIXTURE HISTORY

Pl: 2 Draws: 0		Wins ⚽
Bolton Wanderers	2	4
Fulham	0	1

STARTING LINE-UPS

Jaaskelainen

Hunt   Ben Haim   N'Gotty   Candela

Hierro
Okocha (c)   Speed

Pedersen   Fadiga

Davies

Cole

Boa Morte   Radzinski

Legwinski   Diop

Clark (c)

Bocanegra   Goma   Knight   Rosenior

van der Sar

Poole, Barness, Gardner, Nolan, Vaz Te

Crossley, Pearce, Jensen , John, McBride

Jay-Jay Okocha competes with Tomasz Radzinski

STATISTICS

Fixture		Fixture
5	Shots On Target	3
2	Shots Off Target	9
0	Hit Woodwork	0
3	Caught Offside	0
4	Corners	5
6	Fouls	13

Bolton advanced to the FA Cup Quarter-Finals, as an early Kevin Davies goal proved enough to see off the challenge of Fulham.

Though the game failed to live up to the standard expected when Premiership teams go head-to-head, the decisive moment was something special.

There were 12 minutes on the clock when Davies struck what turned out to be the winner.

A sweeping move saw the ball reach Henrik Pedersen, and from his weighted pass the former Southampton frontman produced a crisp finish.

With a narrow lead to protect, Sam Allardyce's charges began to sit back. This encouraged the visitors to commit more men forward, and they had plenty of chances to equalise before the break.

Luis Boa Morte gets a shot away

EVENT LINE

12	⚽	**Davies (Indirect Free Kick)**
		HALF TIME 1 - 0
62	🔄	**Fadiga (Off) Gardner (On)**
71	🔄	**Pedersen (Off) Nolan (On)**
72	🔄	Legwinski (Off) Jensen (On)
77	🔄	Boa Morte (Off) John (On)
81	🔄	Cole (Off) McBride (On)
85	🔄	**Okocha (Off) Barness (On)**
90	▢	**Nolan (Ung.Conduct)**
90	▢	**Speed (Dissent)**
90	▢	John (Ung.Conduct)
		FULL TIME 1 - 0

> **"I am gutted. We bossed the game, and I thought we did enough to win it."**
>
> **Chris Coleman**

Andrew Cole was unlucky to see a snapshot fly just over, while Papa Bouba Diop also went close from distance. Then, following a poor clearance by Jussi Jaaskelainen, Cole should have done better than flash an effort narrowly wide.

The second period got off to an encouraging start, as both sides threatened to score. Fernando Hierro caused panic in the Fulham defence by delivering two teasing crosses, while Cole produced a venomous drive following a jinking Liam Rosenior run.

Tomasz Radzinski was next to try his luck, forcing a fine diving save from the Bolton custodian. The Trotters then mounted an attack of their own, with Nigeria international Jay-Jay Okocha somehow failing to reach Nicky Hunt's inviting centre.

The last half-hour was a story of near misses, with Pedersen guilty of a particularly glaring one. The Dane was faced with a gaping goal after Okocha got the better of Edwin van der Sar, but his contact was too weak to beat the covering defender.

With time running out, the Cottagers twice went within inches of forcing a replay.

Ricardo Gardner did brilliantly to deny Diop with a last-gasp clearance, and Anthony Barness did likewise to keep Claus Jensen at bay.

Luis **Boa Morte**

Luis Boa Morte was signed by Arsenal in 1997 after Arsène Wenger had watched him represent Portugal in a friendly Under-21 tournament. However, with such tough competition for a regular place at Highbury, David Jones took Luis to Southampton, where the prospect of regular football was more realistic. However, Glenn Hoddle's arrival on the South Coast saw Luis once again spending more time on the bench.

However, Jean Tigana saw enough talent in the forward to bring him for a trial at Fulham. A year-long loan deal followed as Luis took his place among a strike force that would come to terrorise the First Division. He scored 21 goals in Fulham's Championship-winning campaign and was rewarded for his remarkable season with a four-year deal worth £1.7million in summer 2001.

Boa Morte reverted to his preferred position as an attacking left-sided midfielder once the Whites stepped up to the top flight and has wreaked havoc down that left flank ever since.

Voted Player of the Season for 2004/05, the Portugal international's impassioned performances were a vital part of a tough campaign for Fulham. Not only scoring more goals with his left foot than any other player in the Premier League, he also finished the season as the Club's second-most consistent tackler behind Moritz Volz.

MIDFIELDER/FORWARD

PERSONAL INFO

Date of birth	04/08/77
Place of birth	Lisbon
Height	176.5 cm
Weight	78.7 kg
Fulham debut	vs Crewe Alexandra (H)
	12/08/00
Fee	£1.7m
Previous clubs	Sporting Lisbon,
	Arsenal, Southampton

STATS 2004/05

	App	⚽	▢	▣
League	31	8	7	–
FA Cup	5	1	–	–
Carling Cup	3	–	–	–
Total	**39**	**9**	**7**	**–**

Luis Boa Morte

Carlos **Bocanegra**

Although a central defender by trade, for the majority of last season this versatile American international occupied the left-back slot for the Whites.

Brought in from MLS side Chicago Fire in January 2004, Carlos Bocanegra's tough-tackling, no-nonsense style made him the immediate choice to cover for injured full back Jerome Bonnissel.

A regular in the US national side, he will undoubtedly have his sights firmly set on the World Cup in Germany as the new season gets underway.

DEFENDER

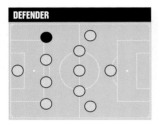

PERSONAL INFO

Date of birth	25/05/79
Place of birth	California
Height	180.5 cm
Weight	79.4 kg
Fulham debut	vs Newcastle United (A)
	19/01/04
Fee	Undisclosed
Previous clubs	Chicago Fire

STATS 2004/05

	App	⚽	▢	■
League	28	1	4	–
FA Cup	4	–	2	–
Carling Cup	3	–	–	–
Total	**35**	**1**	**6**	**–**

Carlos Bocanegra

FORWARD

PERSONAL INFO

Date of birth	15/10/71
Place of birth	Nottingham
Height	178 cm
Weight	81 kg
Fulham debut	vs Manchester City (A)
	14/08/04
Fee	Free
Previous clubs	Arsenal, Fulham (loan),
	Bristol City,
	Newcastle United,
	Manchester United,
	Blackburn Rovers

STATS 2004/05

	App	⚽	☐	■
League	31	12	4	1
FA Cup	5	–	1	–
Carling Cup	3	1	2	–
Total	**39**	**13**	**7**	**1**

Andrew **Cole**

Having spent a period on loan at Fulham in the early 90s as an unknown teenager, Andrew Cole rejoined the Whites last summer having spent the intervening 13 years becoming the second-highest goalscorer in Premiership history. One of the most renowned strikers in England, and with a CV to rival the very best, the former Blackburn striker was looking to start afresh last summer and Fulham provided the opportunity.

Playing as a loan striker for much of last season, Cole scored 12 goals and finished joint fifth highest scorer in the Premiership. Clearly enjoying life at Fulham, he also took the Captain's armband for a spell while Lee Clark was injured.

It was back in 1991 that Cole first came to Craven Cottage on loan from Arsenal. With the Whites then in the Third Division, Cole netted his first ever League goal in the Club's 2-2 draw at Stoke. In August last year, once again back in black and white, he scored his 200th League goal against Bolton.

After leaving Fulham in 1991, Cole went to Bristol City, Newcastle United and Manchester United, where he became a key figure in one of the most successful United sides in history, winning the Premiership, FA Cup and Champions League in 1998/99.

Andrew Cole

GOALKEEPER

PERSONAL INFO

Date of birth	16/04/69
Place of birth	Barnsley
Height	192 cm
Weight	99 kg
Fulham debut	vs Wigan Athletic (A)
	23/09/03
Fee	Undisclosed
Previous clubs	Nottingham Forest,
	Middlesbrough

STATS 2004/05

	App	🟨	🟥	⬛
League	5	1	–	–
FA Cup	–	–	–	–
Carling Cup	3	1	–	–
Total	**8**	**2**	**–**	**–**

Mark **Crossley**

Two incredible performances against Birmingham City and Newcastle United last season summed up the professionalism and sheer stubbornness with which Mark Crossley goes about his job.

Stopping the ball with his hands, arms, legs, feet and even his face at times, Crossley kept Holland international Edwin van der Sar on the bench for a spell between October and November 2004, before an injury saw him lose his place.

Signed in summer 2003 to replace Maik Taylor, Crossley began his career with Nottingham Forest, for whom he made over 370 appearances between 1987 and 2000. Following loan spells with Manchester United and Millwall, the Wales international signed with Middlesbrough in July 2000 before joining Fulham in 2003.

Mark Crossley

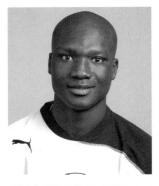

MIDFIELDER

Papa Bouba **Diop**

Comparisons with Patrick Vieira are understandable considering Papa Bouba Diop's incredible debut season for Fulham in 2004/05.

The 6'4" Senegal international's two sublime goals at the Cottage against Chelsea and Manchester United – both exocet rockets from 30 yards – will live long in the memory of everyone there on both nights. His last-minute headed winner against West Brom brought the house down for a third time as the 27-year-old rapidly went about establishing himself as one of the classiest and strongest defensive midfielders in the top flight.

Diop was Chris Coleman's fifth signing of the summer transfer window in July 2004 as he moved from French Le Championnat side, Lens, for an undisclosed fee. An established international, he helped Senegal reach the Quarter-Finals of the African Cup of Nations last year. However, it was his goal that beat France in the opening game of the 2002 World Cup for which Diop will be remembered by most.

PERSONAL INFO

Date of birth	28/01/78
Place of birth	Senegal
Height	194 cm
Weight	94 kg
Fulham debut	vs Manchester City (A)
	14/08/04
Fee	Undisclosed
Previous clubs	Espoir Dakar, Diaraaf
	Dakar, Vevey Sports,
	Neufchatel Xamax,
	Grasshoppers
	Zurich, Lens

STATS 2004/05

	App	⚽	🟨	🟥
League	29	6	7	2
FA Cup	3	1	1	–
Carling Cup	3	–	–	–
Total	**35**	**7**	**8**	**2**

Papa Bouba Diop

Jaroslav **Drobny**

Jaroslav Drobny joined the Club in June after finalising a move that had been on the cards since January 2005, when the Czech goalkeeper signed a pre-agreement contract while with former club Panionios.

The 25-year-old shot-stopper moved from the Greek side for an undisclosed fee, agreeing a three-year deal which will see him at Fulham until 2008.

Drobny said of the move: "I am very happy to get the opportunity to play for Fulham in the Premiership. It is my ambition to compete at the very highest level and I am looking forward to joining the rest of the squad for pre-season training."

One of the most highly rated goalkeepers in the Greek League, Drobny has played in the UEFA Cup for two consecutive seasons, competing against Newcastle and Barcelona among others.

Between 1999-2002, while with SK Ceske – for whom he played prior to joining Panionios – Drobny also made 18 appearances for his national Under-21 side.

GOALKEEPER

PERSONAL INFO	
Date of birth	19/10/79
Place of birth	Pocatky, Czechoslovakia
Height	TBC
Weight	TBC
Fulham debut	—
Fee	Undisclosed
Previous clubs	Ceske Budejovice, Panionios

STATS 2004/05

	App	🗋	▢	■
League	N/A	N/A	N/A	N/A
FA Cup	N/A	N/A	N/A	N/A
Carling Cup	N/A	N/A	N/A	N/A
Total	N/A	N/A	N/A	N/A

Ahmad **Elrich**

Fulham Football Club announced the signing of Australia international midfielder Ahmad Elrich for an undisclosed fee in early June 2005.

Having successfully completed a medical, and subject to the necessary work permit, the three-year deal will see the player at the Club until the summer of 2008.

Formerly of Korean club Busan I'cons, 24-year-old Elrich represented his country at the 2004 Olympic Games in Athens, where he was arguably Australia's best player.

After making his senior national team debut against Venezuela in Caracas during 2004, Elrich has become a regular fixture in the side, playing 12 matches and scoring four goals.

Prior to moving to Korea, Elrich played 120 games and scored 19 goals for Parramatta Power in Australia's National Soccer League, winning a Player of the Match award in the 2004 Grand Final, which his side lost in extra time.

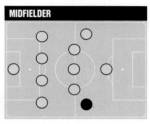

MIDFIELDER

PERSONAL INFO

Date of birth	30/05/81
Place of birth	Sydney, Australia
Height	TBC
Weight	TBC
Fulham debut	—
Fee	Undisclosed
Previous clubs	Parramatta Power, Busan I'cons

STATS 2004/05

	App	⚽	▫	■
League	N/A	N/A	N/A	N/A
FA Cup	N/A	N/A	N/A	N/A
Carling Cup	N/A	N/A	N/A	N/A
Total	N/A	N/A	N/A	N/A

DEFENDER

Alain **Goma**

Alain Goma's career in professional football began at the Academy of French side AJ Auxerre in 1988. He made his League debut in 1991 and a year later was selected for the French Under-21 side. In 1994, Goma and his Auxerre team-mates won the French FA Cup, which also led to a UEFA Cup place.

Goma made over 200 appearances in a 10-year spell with Auxerre before moving to French giants Paris St Germain, where he made 30 appearances and won the Champion's Trophy (French equivalent of the Charity Shield). In 1999 Goma joined Newcastle United, where he became an integral part of the Magpies' defence.

Goma broke Fulham's transfer record in March 2001 when he signed for £4million, and, since his arrival in West London, his composed and elegant style has seen him become a stalwart figure in the centre of the Fulham defence, hence his nickname, "The Rock".

Despite spending most of last season on the physio's bench with a string of injuries, Goma came back in to the side in February and, alongside Zat Knight, re-established a solid central defensive partnership that played a significant part in keeping Fulham out of relegation trouble.

PERSONAL INFO

Date of birth	05/10/72
Place of birth	Sault, France
Height	184 cm
Weight	86.3 kg
Fulham debut	vs Portsmouth (A)
	21/04/01
Fee	£4m
Previous clubs	Auxerre, PSG,
	Newcastle United

STATS 2004/05

	App	⚽	▢	▪
League	16	–	2	–
FA Cup	3	–	–	–
Carling Cup	1	–	–	–
Total	**20**	**–**	**2**	**–**

Collins **John**

With the arrival of Andrew Cole, 2004/05 was always going to be a tough year for Collins John. However, the young Liberian striker proved an invaluable member of the squad, scoring some vital goals, including the opener in the Whites' 2-0 home win over Everton that secured Fulham's mathematical safety in the Premiership.

His performances throughout the season also made the Dutch national team take note. Stepping up from his regular Under-21 spot, 2004-05 also marked his Holland senior-team debut.

The former FC Twente leading scorer joined the Club in January 2004 and overcame injury to score four times in his first eight appearances for the Whites at the tail end of 2003/04.

FORWARD

PERSONAL INFO

Date of birth	07/10/85
Place of birth	Zwandru, Liberia
Height	181.7 cm
Weight	82 kg
Fulham debut	vs Chelsea (A)
	20/03/04
Fee	Undisclosed
Previous clubs	FC Twente

STATS 2004/05

	App	⚽	☐	■
League	27	4	2	–
FA Cup	5	2	2	–
Carling Cup	2	–	–	–
Total	**34**	**6**	**4**	–

Zat **Knight**

The tallest player in the Premier League, Zat Knight has now established himself as one of Chris Coleman's first-choice centre-halves. An almost ever-present last season, his committed defensive style, sheer size and aerial presence helped to shore up the Whites' backline.

Former manager Kevin Keegan signed Knight in 1998 after the youngster returned from a trial period with Portuguese giants Benfica. Still on the books at Midlands amateur side Rushall Olympic, Knight joined Fulham at a cost of nothing more than a few tracksuits donated by Fulham to his former club. With his value measured in the millions today, the Whites' investment was a wise one.

Since then Knight has gone from strength to strength. Under Jean Tigana's guidance he made a number of promising performances during Fulham's first season in the Premier League. However, since Chris Coleman made him a regular in the side, Knight has become one of the Whites' most consistent defenders.

A former England Under-21 international, Knight received his first call-up to the senior England squad for the summer tour of America.

DEFENDER

PERSONAL INFO

Date of birth	02/05/80
Place of birth	Solihull
Height	199.5 cm
Weight	97.2 kg
Fulham debut	vs Northampton (H)
	05/09/00
Fee	Free
Previous clubs	Rushall Olympic

STATS 2004/05

	App	⚽	▢	▩
League	35	1	3	1
FA Cup	5	1	–	–
Carling Cup	2	–	–	–
Total	**42**	**2**	**3**	**1**

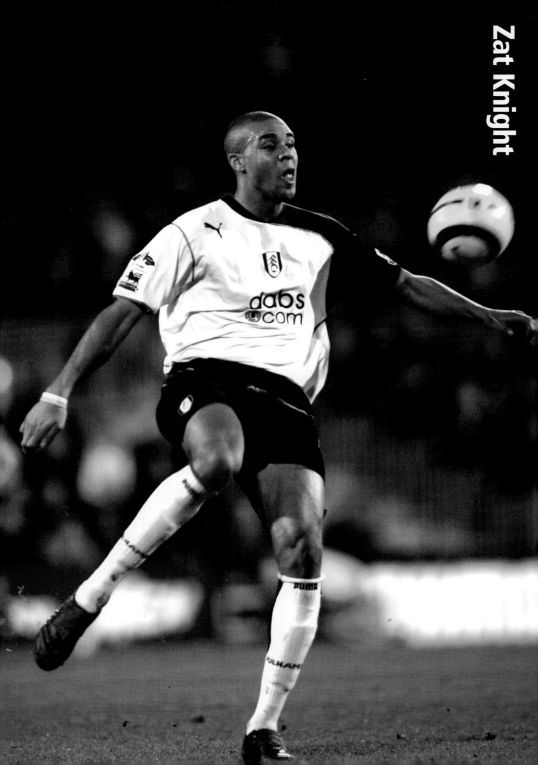

Zat Knight

MIDFIELDER

Sylvain **Legwinski**

Frenchman Sylvain Legwinski put pen to paper at Fulham in a four-year deal worth £3.3million just after the start of the 2001/02 season. He was well known by Jean Tigana, having played under his managerial reign at Monaco. Together with John Collins, Sylvain was part of the successful Monaco side that won the French Championship in 1996/97 and reached the Semi-Finals of the UEFA Cup during the same season. Legwinski joined French giants Bordeaux in January 2000, but jumped at the opportunity to work under Tigana again, this time at Fulham.

A versatile midfielder who can play in front of the back four or in a wide right position, Legwinski adds strength and depth to Fulham's midfield. Although not prolific, Legwinski has the ability to set up and sometimes score vital goals at vital times. Few Fulham fans will ever forget his 95th-minute winner at home against Tottenham during the 2002/03 season when, having gone in 2-0 down at half-time, the team came back to win 3-2.

PERSONAL INFO

Date of birth	10/06/73
Place of birth	Clermont-Ferrand, France
Height	184.9 cm
Weight	73.6 kg
Fulham debut	vs Derby (H) 25/08/01
Fee	£3.3m
Previous clubs	Monaco, Bordeaux

STATS 2004/05

	App	⚽	☐	◼
League	15	1	3	–
FA Cup	5	–	–	–
Carling Cup	1	–	–	–
Total	**21**	**1**	**3**	**–**

FORWARD

Brian **McBride**

Brian McBride scored one of the most important goals of the 2004/05 campaign back in April 2005 when his instinctive overhead strike put Fulham 2-1 up in the crunch match against Portsmouth at Craven Cottage. It was a moment that brought the house down. A goal behind early on, the Whites went on to win 3-1 and took a giant step towards Premiership safety.

Originally from Arlington Heights, Illinois, 33-year-old McBride arrived from Columbus Crew of the MLS in January 2004. While with Columbus he was a seven-time MLS All-Star and the side's all-time leading scorer with 50 goals in 137 games.

A key part of the US national team over many seasons, McBride played a starring role in the 2002 World Cup, scoring the US's winning goals against Portugal and Mexico en route to the Quarter-Finals.

He made his debut for the Whites against Tottenham at Loftus Road and, within eight minutes of his second-half appearance as a substitute, scored the winner in the 2-1 victory.

PERSONAL INFO

Date of birth	19/06/72
Place of birth	Chicago
Height	183.6 cm
Weight	80.2 kg
Fulham debut	vs Tottenham Hotspur (H)
	31/01/04
Fee	Undisclosed
Previous clubs	Columbus Crew,
	Preston North End (loan),
	Everton (loan)

STATS 2004/05

	App	⚽	▢	▮
League	31	6	–	–
FA Cup	2	–	–	–
Carling Cup	3	3	–	–
Total	**36**	**9**	**–**	**–**

Steed **Malbranque**

One of the most influential players in Fulham's recent history, Steed Malbranque joined the club from French League runners-up, Lyon, during summer 2001. Since then he has gone on to become one of the most skillful midfielders in the Premiership.

Having been an almost ever-present in the 2003/04 season, last year's campaign got off to the worst possible start for the Frenchman, as he picked up a persistent injury during pre-season that ruled him out until late September.

Nevertheless, Malbranque made the most of a generally frustrating campaign and by the end was once again in electrifying form, scoring three goals in the last two games.

At international level, Malbranque twice won the French Championship as an Under-15, and was also part of the France side that finished runners-up in the 1996 Under-16 European Championship. He then went on to captain France on their journey to the Final of the 2002 European Under-21 Championships in Switzerland.

MIDFIELDER

PERSONAL INFO

Date of birth	06/01/1980
Place of birth	Mouscron, Belgium
Height	170 cm
Weight	77.1 kg
Fulham debut	vs Manchester United (A) 19/08/01
Fee	£4.5m
Previous clubs	Lyon

STATS 2004/05

	App	⚽	☐	■
League	26	6	–	–
FA Cup	1	–	–	–
Carling Cup	4	1	–	–
Total	**31**	**7**	**–**	**–**

Liam Rosenior

DEFENDER

Moritz **Volz**

Moritz Volz joined the club from Arsenal in the summer of 2003, initially on loan. However, after impressing during the first half of the 2003/04 campaign, Volz put pen to paper on a three-year permanent contract, and, by the end of the season, he was the most consistent tackler in the Premiership.

The German Under 21 international – who is well placed for a spot in the senior team for the World Cup in Germany next summer – began his career with Schalke of the Bundesliga before signing for the Gunners in August 2000. With Lauren and Kolo Toure ahead of him in the Highbury pecking order, however, Volz's chances of breaking into the first team were slim. He consequently spent the second half of 2002/03 on loan at Wimbledon.

Having been an almost ever-present in the Fulham team throughout 2003/04, Volz maintained his status as first-choice right-back last season, although rising young star Liam Rosenior made him work for his place.

Volz's first Fulham goal also came last season when he scored the opener in the Whites' 2-0 win over Watford in the FA Cup Third Round Replay at Craven Cottage in January.

PERSONAL INFO

Date of birth	21/01/83
Place of birth	Siegen, Germany
Height	178.5 cm
Weight	78.3 kg
Fulham debut	vs Middlesbrough (H)
	16/08/03
Fee	Undisclosed
Previous clubs	Schalke, Arsenal

STATS 2004/05

	App	⚽	▢	▮
League	31	–	5	–
FA Cup	2	1	–	–
Carling Cup	3	–	1	–
Total	**36**	**1**	**6**	–

Moritz Volz

Ricardo **Batista**

19-year-old Ricardo Batista joined Fulham last season from Portuguese side Vitoria FC Setubal.

The highly rated goalkeeper currently plays in Portugal's Under-20 side, having also formerly played for the Under-19s.

A valuable addition to the squad, he played in several Reserve games last season, his quick reactions and good judgment showing the obvious potential he has and demonstrating why he is so well respected in Portugal.

PERSONAL INFO	
Position	Goalkeeper
Date of birth	19/11/86
Place of birth	Portugal
Height	TBC
Weight	TBC
Fulham debut	—
Fee	Undisclosed
Previous clubs	Vitoria FC Setubal

Ismael **Ehui**

A powerful striker, Ismael Ehui is originally from Paris. He moved with his parents to London, where Fulham scouts in North London picked him up.

He has great potential as a forward, with excellent technique on both his left and right feet, strength in the air and a good turn of pace. Very much a player in the Ian Wright mould.

A huge talent for the future, Ehui was a key part of the Reserve team last season and even made the First Team for a couple of the 04/05 pre-season friendlies. One to keep an eye on.

PERSONAL INFO	
Position	Forward
Date of birth	10/12/86
Place of birth	Lille, France
Height	168.5 cm
Weight	65.2 kg
Fulham debut	—
Fee	N/A
Previous clubs	Fulham Academy

Elvis **Hammond**

Elvis Hammond joined Fulham's Academy at Under 16 level and has been a consistent goalscorer in the years since. However, despite breaking in to the First Team at the tail end of the 2002/03 season (during which he was top scorer in the Premier Reserve League South with 13 goals), an injury-stricken 2003/04 meant that he largely watched from the sidelines.

Last season was a different story though, as, having regained his fitness, he provided a memorable assist for Brian McBride to level the scores at 1-1 in Fulham's Carling Cup match against Chelsea at Craven Cottage. Following that, the energetic frontman went on loan to Dutch side RBC Roosendaal, where he proved a success.

A powerful and pacy striker with a natural eye for goal, his Fulham First Team debut came in 2000/01, when he appeared as a substitute in the League Cup game at Chesterfield.

Hammond has dual nationality, having been born in Ghana to a British mother, and has played with some of the big Ghanaian names, such as Marcel Desailly, George Weah, Roger Milla and Abedi Pele.

PERSONAL INFO	
Position	Forward
Date of birth	06/10/80
Place of birth	Accra, Ghana
Height	177 cm
Weight	71 kg
Fulham debut	vs Chesterfield (A)
	19/09/00
Fee	N/A
Previous clubs	Fulham Academy

Dean **Leacock**

Dean Leacock is a quick, strong defender with good technique and excellent distribution. He can occupy either a full back or a centre half role. A local boy, who originally hails from Thornton Heath, he made his debut for Fulham two seasons ago in a Fourth Round Worthington Cup game away at Wigan.

Predominantly right-footed, Leacock also has a useful left foot and is an expert at long diagonal passes.

Although blighted by injury for large periods of last season, Leacock did enjoy a successful loan spell at Coventry City and could well be fighting for a First Team birth this term.

PERSONAL INFO	
Position	Defender
Date of birth	10/06/84
Place of birth	Croydon
Height	189 cm
Weight	78 kg
Fulham debut	vs Wigan Athletic (H)
	04/12/02
Fee	N/A
Previous clubs	Fulham Academy

Neale **McDermott**

Neale McDermott joined Fulham from Newcastle United in January 2003.

Son of Liverpool great, Terry McDermott, the former England Under-18 international provides an intelligent head in midfield and can get forward well to support the front men. He played an important role in the Reserve team last season.

PERSONAL INFO	
Position	Midfielder
Date of birth	08/03/85
Place of birth	Newcastle-upon-Tyne
Height	181.5 cm
Weight	71.3 kg
Fulham debut	—
Fee	Undisclosed
Previous clubs	Newcastle United

Darren **Pratley**

Twenty-year-old Darren Pratley made his debut for the First Team in the Carling Cup game against Wigan in September 2003 and went on to make an appearance in the League game against Charlton at The Valley in November of the same year.

A central midfield player, he is another Academy graduate who joined Fulham's youth set-up from Arsenal and who is surely only being kept out of the First Team by the number of more experienced central midfield players who are already established in the senior squad.

He spent much of the second half of last season on loan at Brentford, where he enjoyed a successful spell in the first team. On his return to Fulham, Pratley told fulhamfc.com: "I've really enjoyed the spell away – I've learned a lot from it. But I'll be back for pre-season, hopefully making a push for a First Team place here."

PERSONAL INFO	
Position	Midfielder
Date of birth	22/04/85
Place of birth	Barking
Height	186.5 cm
Weight	72.6 kg
Fulham debut	vs Wigan Athletic (A)
	29/09/03
Fee	N/A
Previous clubs	Arsenal,
	Fulham Academy

Michael **Timlin**

A hugely talented central midfielder, Michael Timlin suffered a frustrating 2003/04 campaign after a back condition then a broken metatarsal effectively ruled him out for the whole season.

Timlin started his Fulham career as a left winger, but was converted to central midfield by Fulham's then Academy Director, Steve Kean. The switch paid remarkable dividends for the player, who made rapid progress through the Academy's ranks and moved on to the international stage with the Republic of Ireland before running into injury problems.

Timlin maintained a philosophical outlook during his layoff and made a return to competitive football last season with the Reserves.

PERSONAL INFO	
Position	Midfielder
Date of birth	19/03/85
Place of birth	Lambeth
Height	175.5 cm
Weight	74.5 kg
Fulham debut	vs Boston United (A)
	22/09/04
Fee	N/A
Previous clubs	Fulham Academy

Robert **Watkins**

A left-sided central defender, Robert Watkins joined Fulham's Academy as a schoolboy. Though he originally came to the Club as a left winger, he was converted to a defender early on after Fulham's coaching staff spotted his natural defensive abilities.

Watkins is a good reader of the game and plays with a style reminiscent of former Fulham Captain, Andy Melville.

"He's not a flash player – he does his job with the minimum of fuss," said former Fulham Reserve team manager, Paul Nevin. "You'll rarely see him have a bad game, so in that respect he's a very dependable player. Technically, he's very good. He can play nice short passes, but he's also capable of playing accurate longer balls."

PERSONAL INFO	
Position	Defender
Date of birth	14/10/85
Place of birth	Sutton
Height	TBC
Weight	TBC
Fulham debut	—
Fee	N/A
Previous clubs	Fulham Academy

Arsenal

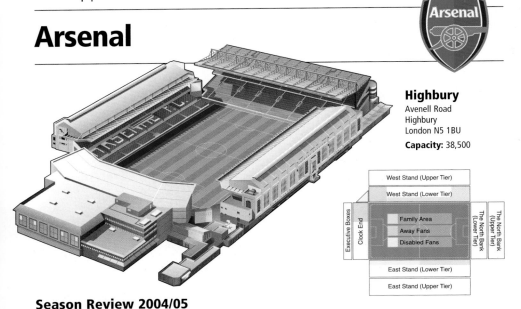

Highbury
Avenell Road
Highbury
London N5 1BU

Capacity: 38,500

West Stand (Upper Tier)

West Stand (Lower Tier)

Executive Boxes	Clock End	Family Area	The North Bank (Lower Tier)	The North Bank (Upper Tier)
		Away Fans		
		Disabled Fans		

East Stand (Lower Tier)

East Stand (Upper Tier)

Season Review 2004/05

Having enjoyed an incredible unbeaten run to the Premiership title the previous season, Arsenal had to settle for second place this time around.

The Gunners began their League campaign in blistering form, winning 3-0 at Craven Cottage in September, but came unstuck after an October defeat at Old Trafford. Arsène Wenger's men took time to recover from this setback, though they gained revenge by beating their great rivals in the FA Cup Final.

FINAL POSITION 2004/05

	P	W	D	L	F	A	GD	Pts
01 Chelsea	38	29	8	1	72	15	57	95
02 Arsenal	38	25	8	5	87	36	51	83
03 Manchester United	38	22	11	5	58	26	32	77

GOAL BREAKDOWN 2004/05

Time (mins)	For	Against
0-15	8 (9%)	1 (3%)
16-30	12 (14%)	3 (8%)
31-45	18 (21%)	6 (17%)
46-60	14 (16%)	7 (19%)
61-75	20 (23%)	9 (25%)
76-90+	15 (17%)	10 (28%)

RECENT MEETINGS

Date	Competition	Result	Attendance
26/12/04	League	Arsenal 2-0 Fulham	38,047
11/09/04	League	Fulham 0-3 Arsenal	21,681
09/05/04	League	Fulham 0-1 Arsenal	18,102
30/11/03	League	Arsenal 0-0 Fulham	38,063
01/02/03	League	Arsenal 2-1 Fulham	38,050

USEFUL INFORMATION

Nickname	The Gunners
Manager	Arsène Wenger
Chairman	Peter Hill-Wood
Telephone	020 7704 4000
Ticket Office	020 7704 4040
Club Shop	020 7704 4120
Website	www.arsenal.com

ALL-TIME RECORD VS FULHAM

Played	Won	Drawn	Lost	For	Against
37	26	6	5	81	46

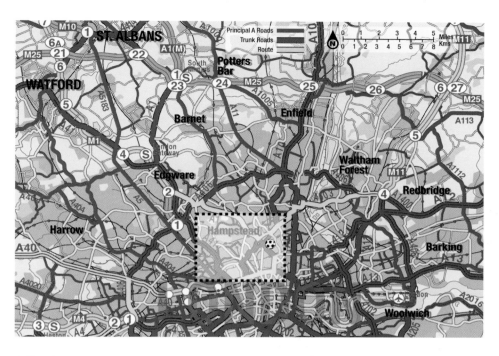

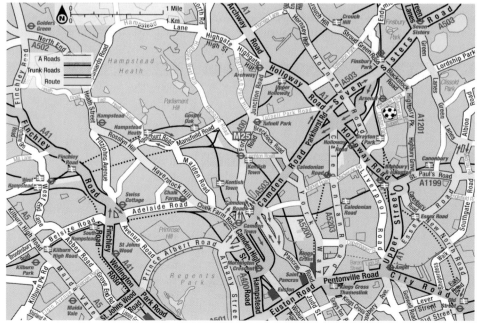

Aston Villa

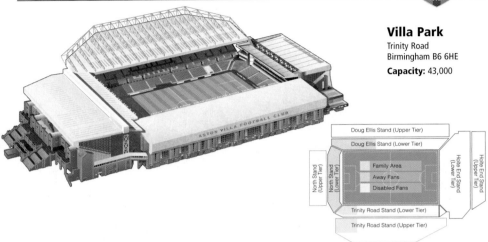

Villa Park
Trinity Road
Birmingham B6 6HE
Capacity: 43,000

Season Review 2004/05

It was a fairly uneventful season at Villa Park, as David O'Leary's side finished in mid-table. The fans felt frustrated by a perceived lack of investment by chairman Doug Ellis, though this gave an opportunity to youngsters such as Steven Davis and Luke Moore. Two defeats at the hands of bitter local rivals Birmingham did little to lift the mood on the terraces, though Lee Hendrie did net some spectacular goals.

FINAL POSITION 2004/05

	P	W	D	L	F	A	GD	Pts
09 Tottenham Hotspur	38	14	10	14	47	41	6	52
10 Aston Villa	38	12	11	15	45	52	-7	47
11 Charlton Athletic	38	12	10	16	42	58	-16	46

RECENT MEETINGS

Date	Competition	Result	Attendance
02/02/05	League	Fulham 1-1 Aston Villa	17,624
23/10/04	League	Aston Villa 2-0 Fulham	34,460
11/02/04	League	Fulham 1-2 Aston Villa	16,153
28/12/03	League	Aston Villa 3-0 Fulham	35,617
08/02/03	League	Fulham 2-1 Aston Villa	17,092

ALL-TIME RECORD VS FULHAM

Played	Won	Drawn	Lost	For	Against
46	17	13	16	72	64

GOAL BREAKDOWN 2004/05

Time (mins)	For	Against
0-15	6 (13%)	10 (19%)
16-30	9 (20%)	17 (33%)
31-45	6 (13%)	8 (15%)
46-60	6 (13%)	4 (8%)
61-75	10 (22%)	8 (15%)
76-90+	8 (18%)	5 (10%)

USEFUL INFORMATION

Nickname	The Villans
Manager	David O'Leary
Chairman	Doug Ellis
Telephone	0121 327 2299
Ticket Office	0121 327 5353
Club Shop	0121 327 5353
Website	www.avfc.co.uk

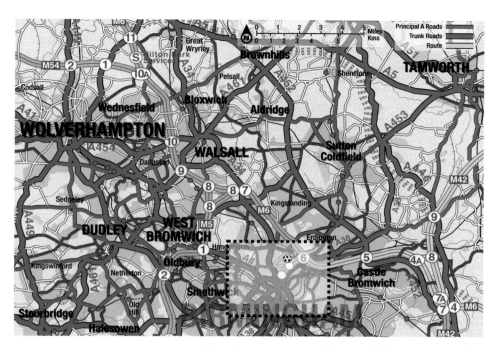

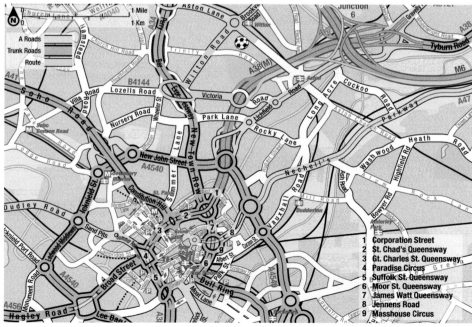

1 Corporation Street
2 St. Chad's Queensway
3 Gt. Charles St. Queensway
4 Paradise Circus
5 Suffolk St. Queensway
6 Moor St. Queensway
7 James Watt Queensway
8 Jennens Road
9 Masshouse Circus

Birmingham City

St Andrew's Stadium

Birmingham B9 4NH
Capacity: 30,016

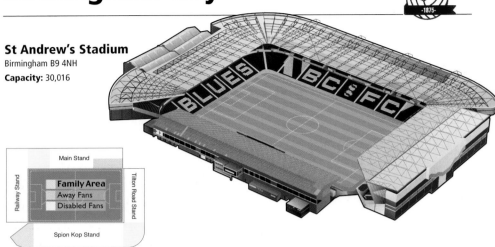

Main Stand

Railway Stand

Family Area
Away Fans
Disabled Fans

Tilton Road Stand

Spion Kop Stand

Season Review 2004/05

As a Birmingham supporter, you didn't know what to expect during 2004/05. A return of just 14 points from the opening 16 games brought with it the threat of relegation, before four straight wins catapulted Steve Bruce's men up the table. The last victory of this run came against Fulham, but a month later Chris Coleman's side won at St Andrew's to inflict a fourth consecutive defeat on their hosts.

FINAL POSITION 2004/05

	P	W	D	L	F	A	GD	Pts
11 Charlton Athletic	38	12	10	16	42	58	-16	46
12 Birmingham City	38	11	12	15	40	46	-6	45
13 Fulham	38	12	8	18	52	60	-8	44

RECENT MEETINGS

Date	Competition	Result	Attendance
22/01/05	League	Birmingham City 1-2 Fulham	28,512
28/12/04	League	Fulham 2-3 Birmingham City	18,706
27/10/04	League Cup	Birmingham City 0-1 Fulham	26,371
03/04/04	League	Fulham 0-0 Birmingham City	14,667
14/09/03	League	Birmingham City 2-2 Fulham	27,250

ALL-TIME RECORD VS FULHAM

Played	Won	Drawn	Lost	For	Against
74	28	23	23	106	111

GOAL BREAKDOWN 2004/05

Time (mins)	For	Against
0-15	8 (20%)	5 (11%)
16-30	6 (15%)	4 (9%)
31-45	8 (20%)	7 (15%)
46-60	6 (15%)	8 (17%)
61-75	6 (15%)	9 (20%)
76-90+	6 (15%)	13 (28%)

USEFUL INFORMATION

Nickname	The Blues
Manager	Steve Bruce
Chairman	David Gold
Telephone	0871 226 1875
Ticket Office	0871 226 1875
Club Shop	0871 226 1875
Website	www.bcfc.com

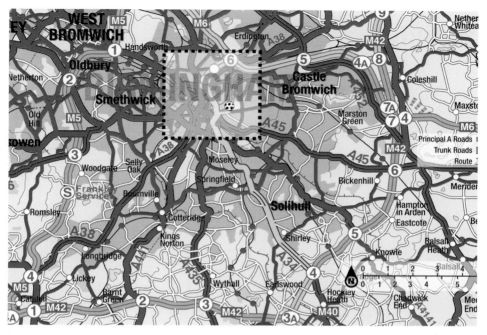

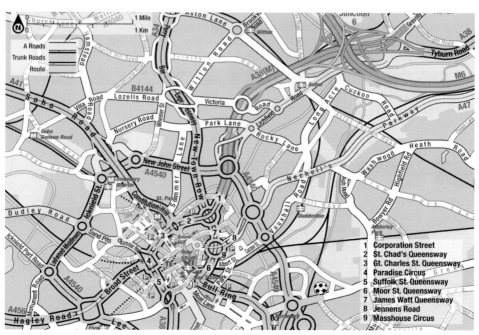

1 Corporation Street
2 St. Chad's Queensway
3 Gt. Charles St. Queensway
4 Paradise Circus
5 Suffolk St. Queensway
6 Moor St. Queensway
7 James Watt Queensway
8 Jennens Road
9 Masshouse Circus

Blackburn Rovers

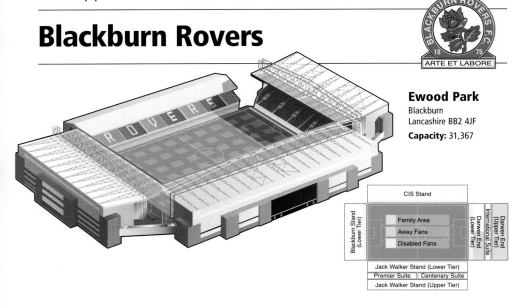

Ewood Park
Blackburn
Lancashire BB2 4JF
Capacity: 31,367

CIS Stand

Blackburn Stand (Lower Tier)			
Family Area		Darwen End (Lower Tier)	Darwen End International Suite (Upper Tier)
Away Fans			
Disabled Fans			

Jack Walker Stand (Lower Tier)
Premier Suite | Centenary Suite
Jack Walker Stand (Upper Tier)

Season Review 2004/05

Former Rover Mark Hughes succeeded Graeme Souness at Ewood Park and immediately set about increasing his side's defensive resolve. Though their style won them few friends, 15 clean sheets helped secure Blackburn's Premiership survival with weeks to spare, while the Lancashire side also reached the last four in the FA Cup. A 2-0 victory at Craven Cottage in November ended an eight-game winless run and was a pivotal moment in Rovers' season.

FINAL POSITION 2004/05

	P	W	D	L	F	A	GD	Pts
14 Newcastle United	38	10	14	14	47	57	-10	44
15 Blackburn Rovers	38	9	15	14	32	43	-11	42
16 Portsmouth	38	10	9	19	43	59	-16	39

GOAL BREAKDOWN 2004/05

Time (mins)	For	Against
0-15	6 (19%)	4 (9%)
16-30	5 (16%)	4 (9%)
31-45	4 (13%)	11 (26%)
46-60	6 (19%)	11 (26%)
61-75	8 (25%)	3 (7%)
76-90+	3 (9%)	10 (23%)

RECENT MEETINGS

Date	Competition	Result	Attendance
07/05/05	League	Blackburn Rovers 1-3 Fulham	18,991
27/11/04	League	Fulham 0-2 Blackburn Rovers	19,103
12/04/04	League	Fulham 3-4 Blackburn Rovers	13,981
28/09/03	League	Blackburn Rovers 0-2 Fulham	21,985
07/04/03	League	Fulham 0-4 Blackburn Rovers	14,017

USEFUL INFORMATION

Nickname	Rovers
Manager	Mark Hughes
Chairman	John Williams
Telephone	08701 113 232
Ticket Office	08701 123 456
Club Shop	01254 296 262
Website	www.rovers.co.uk

ALL-TIME RECORD VS FULHAM

Played	Won	Drawn	Lost	For	Against
71	29	19	23	108	98

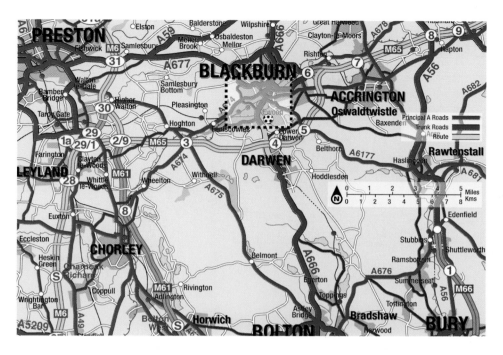

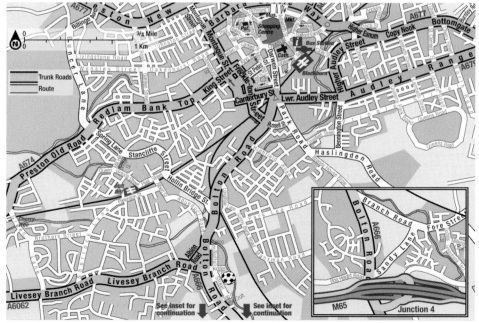

Bolton Wanderers

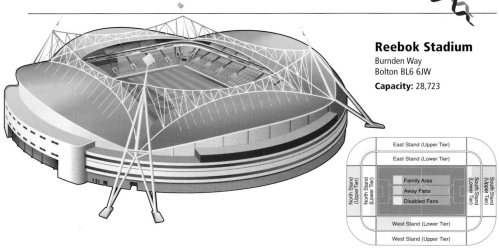

Reebok Stadium
Burnden Way
Bolton BL6 6JW
Capacity: 28,723

East Stand (Upper Tier)	
East Stand (Lower Tier)	
North Stand (Upper Tier) / North Stand (Lower Tier)	Family Area / Away Fans / Disabled Fans	South Stand (Lower Tier) / South Stand (Upper Tier)
West Stand (Lower Tier)	
West Stand (Upper Tier)	

Season Review 2004/05

Sam Allardyce guided Bolton into Europe for the first time in their history. Playing a direct brand of football that utilised the aerial strengths of Kevin Davies, few teams could cope with the power and commitment of the Trotters. Arsenal and Liverpool were beaten at the Reebok Stadium, while no other team netted twice in a Premiership game at Stamford Bridge. It was Bolton who ended Fulham's interest in the FA Cup.

FINAL POSITION 2004/05

	P	W	D	L	F	A	GD	Pts
05 Liverpool	38	17	7	14	52	41	11	58
06 Bolton Wanderers	38	16	10	12	49	44	5	58
07 Middlesbrough	38	14	13	11	53	46	7	55

RECENT MEETINGS

Date	Competition	Result	Attendance
09/04/05	League	Bolton Wanderers 3-1 Fulham	25,493
19/02/05	FA Cup	Bolton Wanderers 1-0 Fulham	16,151
21/08/04	League	Fulham 2-0 Bolton Wanderers	17,541
15/05/04	League	Bolton Wanderers 0-2 Fulham	27,383
06/12/03	League	Fulham 2-1 Bolton Wanderers	14,393

ALL-TIME RECORD VS FULHAM

Played	Won	Drawn	Lost	For	Against
67	28	18	21	91	89

GOAL BREAKDOWN 2004/05

Time (mins)	For	Against
0-15	6 (12%)	6 (14%)
16-30	9 (18%)	3 (7%)
31-45	8 (16%)	7 (16%)
46-60	10 (20%)	7 (16%)
61-75	8 (16%)	11 (25%)
76-90+	8 (16%)	10 (23%)

USEFUL INFORMATION

Nickname	The Trotters
Manager	Sam Allardyce
Chairman	Phil Gartside
Telephone	01204 673 673
Ticket Office	0871 871 2932
Club Shop	01204 673 650
Website	www.bwfc.co.uk

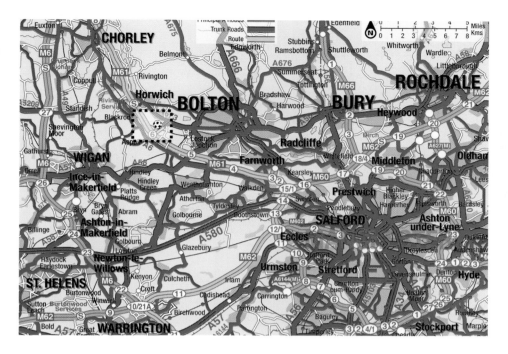

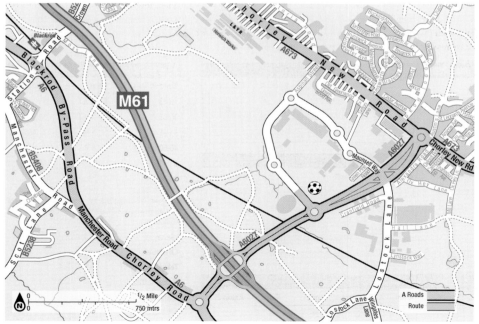

Charlton Athletic

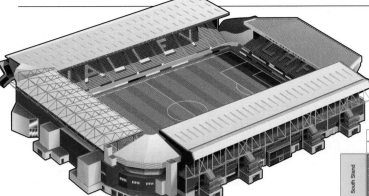

The Valley
Floyd Road
Charlton
London SE7 8BL
Capacity: 27,116

West Stand (Upper Tier) | NorthWest Quadrant
West Stand (Lower Tier)

South Stand

Family Area
Away Fans
Disabled Fans

North Stand

East Stand | NorthEast Quadrant

Season Review 2004/05

Once again, Charlton enjoyed an excellent campaign until mid-March. Having beaten Tottenham to go seventh in the table, the Addicks embarked on their traditional end-of-season slump. Just three points were collected from the final nine games, a sequence of results that saw the men from The Valley slip down into 11th place. Full-back Luke Young was a star performer, earning his first England cap on the May tour to America.

FINAL POSITION 2004/05

	P	W	D	L	F	A	GD	Pts
10 Aston Villa	38	12	11	15	45	52	-7	47
11 Charlton Athletic	38	12	10	16	42	58	-16	46
12 Birmingham City	38	11	12	15	40	46	-6	45

GOAL BREAKDOWN 2004/05

Time (mins)	For	Against
0-15	5 (12%)	7 (12%)
16-30	11 (26%)	3 (5%)
31-45	5 (12%)	9 (16%)
46-60	7 (17%)	15 (26%)
61-75	5 (12%)	13 (22%)
76-90+	9 (21%)	11 (19%)

RECENT MEETINGS

Date	Competition	Result	Attendance
05/03/05	League	Fulham 0-0 Charlton Athletic	18,290
20/12/04	League	Charlton Athletic 2-1 Fulham	26,108
24/04/04	League	Fulham 2-0 Charlton Athletic	16,585
08/11/03	League	Charlton Athletic 3-1 Fulham	26,344
11/05/03	League	Charlton Athletic 0-1 Fulham	26,108

USEFUL INFORMATION

Nickname	The Addicks
Manager	Alan Curbishley
Chairman	Richard Murray
Telephone	020 8333 4000
Ticket Office	020 8333 4010
Club Shop	020 8333 4035
Website	www.cafc.co.uk

ALL-TIME RECORD VS FULHAM

Played	Won	Drawn	Lost	For	Against
60	21	19	20	83	75

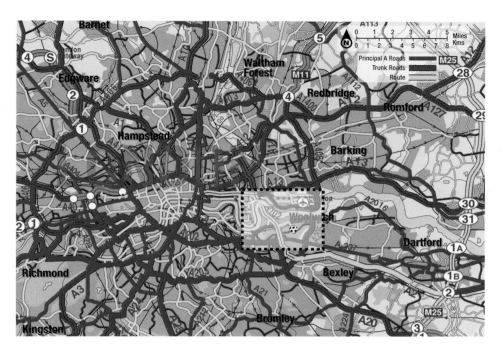

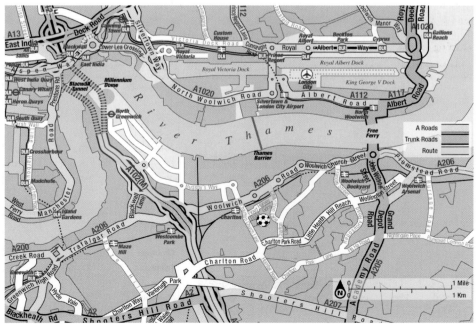

The Opposition

Chelsea

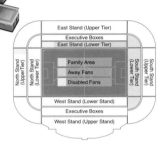

Stamford Bridge

Fulham Road
London SW6 1HS
Capacity: 42,449

Season Review 2004/05

New manager José Mourinho led Chelsea to a first top-flight title in 50 years. The Stamford Bridge side suffered just one League defeat – at Manchester City in October – and finished the season with a Premiership record 95 points. The trophy was the second of the Roman Abramovich era, joining the Carling Cup in the cabinet. A narrow Quarter-Final victory at Craven Cottage was an important step on the way to Cardiff.

FINAL POSITION 2004/05

		P	W	D	L	F	A	GD	Pts
01	Chelsea	38	29	8	1	72	15	57	95
02	Arsenal	38	25	8	5	87	36	51	83
03	Manchester United	38	22	11	5	58	26	32	77

GOAL BREAKDOWN 2004/05

Time (mins)	For	Against
0-15	7 (10%)	4 (27%)
16-30	11 (15%)	1 (7%)
31-45	12 (17%)	3 (20%)
46-60	11 (15%)	3 (20%)
61-75	12 (17%)	3 (20%)
76-90+	19 (26%)	1 (7%)

RECENT MEETINGS

Date	Competition	Result	Attendance
23/04/05	League	Chelsea 3-1 Fulham	42,081
30/11/04	League Cup	Fulham 1-2 Chelsea	14,531
13/11/04	League	Fulham 1-4 Chelsea	21,877
20/03/04	League	Chelsea 2-1 Fulham	41,169
20/12/03	League	Fulham 0-1 Chelsea	18,244

ALL-TIME RECORD VS FULHAM

Played	Won	Drawn	Lost	For	Against
61	35	18	8	101	57

USEFUL INFORMATION

Nickname	The Blues
Manager	José Mourinho
Chairman	Bruce Buck
Telephone	0870 300 1212
Ticket Office	0870 300 2322
Club Shop	0870 300 1212
Website	www.chelseafc.com

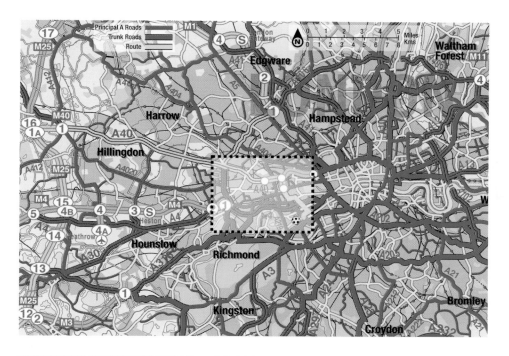

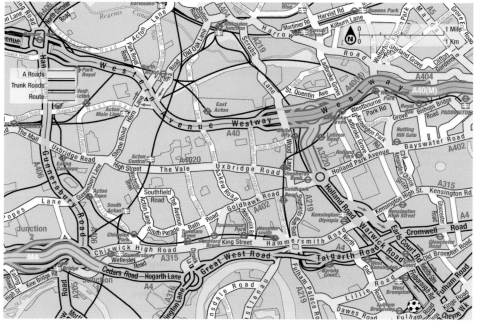

Everton

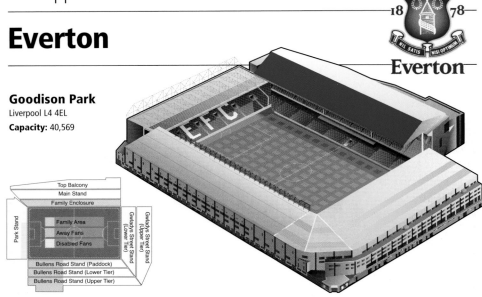

Goodison Park

Liverpool L4 4EL

Capacity: 40,569

Season Review 2004/05

Against all odds, David Moyes guided Everton to fourth position and a place in the 2005/06 Champions League.

Having finished just above the relegation zone the previous season, and with star player Wayne Rooney moving to Manchester United in August, things had looked bleak for the Toffees. But with summer signing Tim Cahill in inspirational form, the Goodison Park side collected 40 points from their first 19 matches and never looked back.

FINAL POSITION 2004/05

	P	W	D	L	F	A	GD	Pts
03 Manchester United	38	22	11	5	58	26	32	77
04 Everton	38	18	7	13	45	46	-1	61
05 Liverpool	38	17	7	14	52	41	11	58

GOAL BREAKDOWN 2004/05

Time (mins)	For	Against
0-15	5 (11%)	7 (15%)
16-30	4 (9%)	7 (15%)
31-45	5 (11%)	8 (17%)
46-60	8 (18%)	10 (22%)
61-75	11 (24%)	8 (17%)
76-90+	12 (27%)	6 (13%)

RECENT MEETINGS

Date	Competition	Result	Attendance
30/04/05	League	Fulham 2-0 Everton	21,881
20/11/04	League	Everton 1-0 Fulham	34,763
04/02/04	FA Cup	Fulham 2-1 Everton	11,551
25/01/04	FA Cup	Everton 1-1 Fulham	27,862
10/01/04	League	Fulham 2-1 Everton	17,103

USEFUL INFORMATION

Nickname	The Toffees
Manager	David Moyes
Chairman	Bill Kenwright
Telephone	0151 330 2200
Ticket Office	0870 442 1878
Club Shop	0151 330 2030
Website	www.evertonfc.com

ALL-TIME RECORD VS FULHAM

Played	Won	Drawn	Lost	For	Against
41	16	11	14	60	48

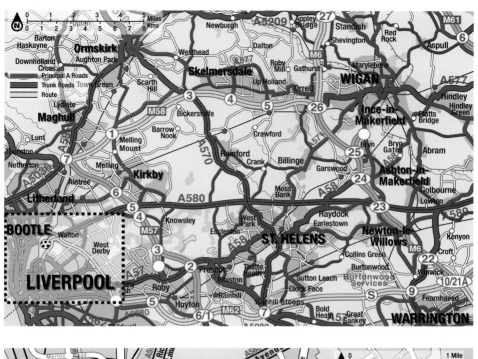

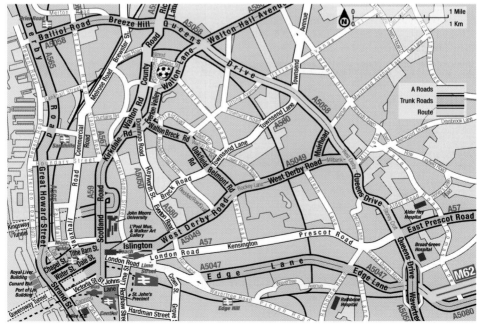

Liverpool

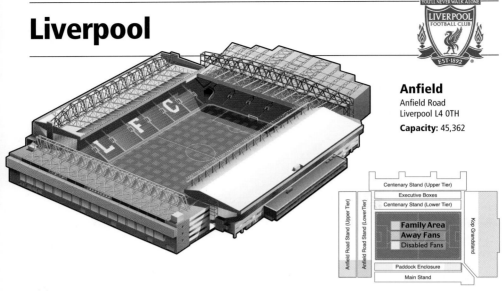

Anfield
Anfield Road
Liverpool L4 0TH
Capacity: 45,362

Centenary Stand (Upper Tier)

Executive Boxes

Centenary Stand (Lower Tier)

Family Area

Away Fans

Disabled Fans

Paddock Enclosure

Main Stand

Anfield Road Stand (Upper Tier)

Anfield Road Stand (Lower Tier)

Kop Grandstand

Season Review 2004/05

Despite a disappointing Premiership campaign that saw the Anfield side lose 14 games and finish fifth, everything went right in Europe.

Rafael Benitez marked his first season in charge by guiding Liverpool to victory in the Champions League, as the club lifted the European Cup for a fifth time. Having beaten Juventus and Chelsea on their way to the Final, the Merseysiders then recovered from a three-goal interval deficit to beat AC Milan on penalties in Istanbul.

FINAL POSITION 2004/05

	P	W	D	L	F	A	GD	Pts
04 Everton	38	18	7	13	45	46	-1	61
05 Liverpool	38	17	7	14	52	41	11	58
06 Bolton Wanderers	38	16	10	12	49	44	5	58

GOAL BREAKDOWN 2004/05

Time (mins)	For	Against
0-15	3 (6%)	3 (7%)
16-30	9 (17%)	10 (24%)
31-45	10 (19%)	11 (27%)
46-60	11 (21%)	3 (7%)
61-75	10 (19%)	7 (17%)
76-90+	9 (17%)	7 (17%)

RECENT MEETINGS

Date	Competition	Result	Attendance
05/02/05	League	Liverpool 3-1 Fulham	43,534
16/10/04	League	Fulham 2-4 Liverpool	21,884
17/04/04	League	Liverpool 0-0 Fulham	42,042
02/11/03	League	Fulham 1-2 Liverpool	17,682
12/04/03	League	Liverpool 2-0 Fulham	42,120

USEFUL INFORMATION

Nickname	The Reds
Manager	Rafael Benitez
Chairman	David Moores
Telephone	0151 263 2361
Ticket Office	0870 220 2151
Club Shop	0870 600 0532
Website	www.liverpoolfc.tv

ALL-TIME RECORD VS FULHAM

Played	Won	Drawn	Lost	For	Against
49	28	14	7	104	52

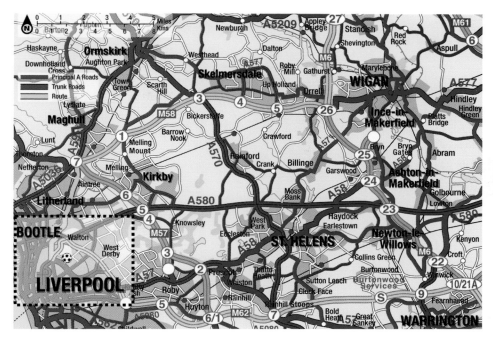

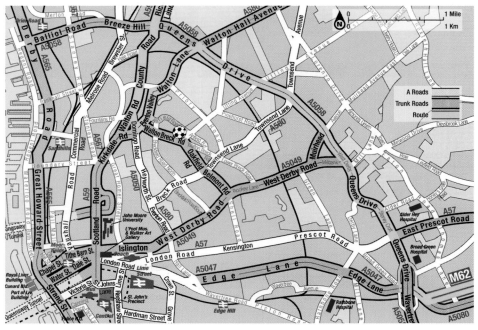

Manchester City

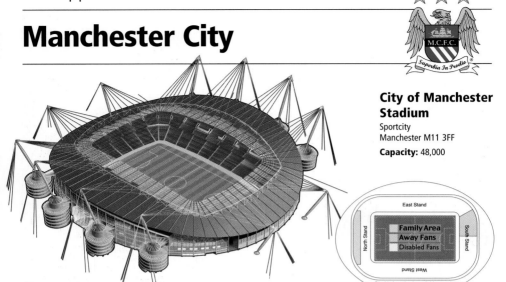

City of Manchester Stadium

Sportcity
Manchester M11 3FF

Capacity: 48,000

East Stand

North Stand

Family Area
Away Fans
Disabled Fans

South Stand

West Stand

Disabled seating is available at various points around the stadium

Season Review 2004/05

A solid, if unspectacular, season under the guidance of Kevin Keegan almost yielded an improbable UEFA Cup place after Stuart Pearce took over. The new man did enough in his caretaker role to secure a permanent appointment, but was left disappointed on the final day after Robbie Fowler's failure to convert a last-gasp penalty against Middlesbrough cost his side a place in Europe.

FINAL POSITION 2004/05

		P	W	D	L	F	A	GD	Pts
07	Middlesbrough	38	14	13	11	53	46	7	55
08	Manchester City	38	13	13	12	47	39	8	52
09	Tottenham Hotspur	38	14	10	14	47	41	6	52

GOAL BREAKDOWN 2004/05

Time (mins)	For	Against
0-15	10 (21%)	8 (21%)
16-30	6 (13%)	4 (10%)
31-45	12 (26%)	2 (5%)
46-60	6 (13%)	8 (21%)
61-75	3 (6%)	8 (21%)
76-90+	10 (21%)	9 (23%)

RECENT MEETINGS

Date	Competition	Result	Attendance
16/04/05	League	Fulham 1-1 Manchester City	21,796
14/08/04	League	Manchester City 1-1 Fulham	44,026
27/03/04	League	Manchester City 0-0 Fulham	46,522
20/09/03	League	Fulham 2-2 Manchester City	16,124
29/01/03	League	Manchester City 4-1 Fulham	33,260

USEFUL INFORMATION

Nickname	The Citizens
Manager	Stuart Pearce
Chairman	John Wardle
Telephone	0161 231 3200
Ticket Office	0870 062 1894
Club Shop	0870 062 1894
Website	www.mcfc.co.uk

ALL-TIME RECORD VS FULHAM

Played	Won	Drawn	Lost	For	Against
44	20	11	13	91	71

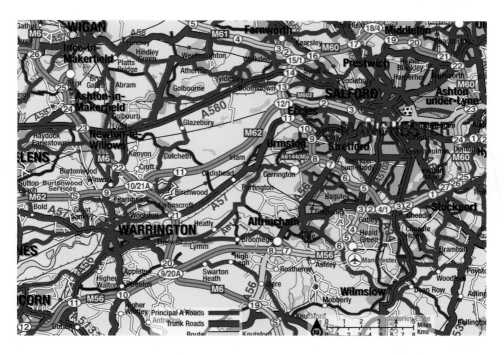

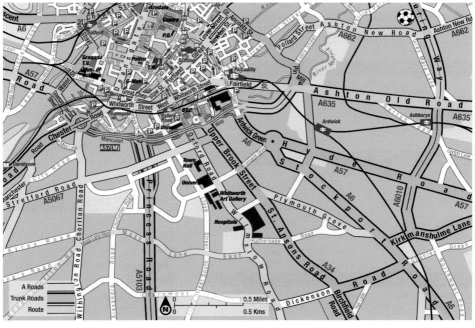

The Opposition

Manchester United

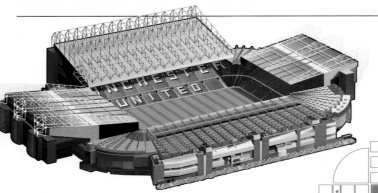

Old Trafford

Sir Matt Busby Way
Old Trafford
Manchester M16 0RA
Capacity: 68,190

| North Stand (Tier 3) |
| Executive Boxes |
| North Stand (Upper Tier) |
| Executive Boxes |
| North Stand (Lower Tier) |

West Stand (Upper Tier)	Executive Boxes	West Stand (Lower Tier)	Family Area	East Stand (Lower Tier)	Executive Boxes	East Stand (Upper Tier)
			Away Fans			
			Disabled Fans			

| South Stand |
| Executive Boxes |

Season Review 2004/05

Defeat in the FA Cup Final meant that Manchester United ended the season without a trophy. Sir Alex Ferguson's side finished a distant third in the Premiership and lost out to Champions Chelsea in the Carling Cup Semi-Finals. Most supporters were more worried about events taking place off the pitch, however, as American businessman Malcolm Glazer took over the club after buying more than 75% of its shares.

FINAL POSITION 2004/05

	P	W	D	L	F	A	GD	Pts
02 Arsenal	38	25	8	5	87	36	51	83
03 Manchester United	38	22	11	5	58	26	32	77
04 Everton	38	18	7	13	45	46	-1	61

RECENT MEETINGS

Date	Competition	Result	Attendance
19/03/05	League	Manchester United 1-0 Fulham	67,959
13/12/04	League	Fulham 1-1 Manchester United	21,940
06/03/04	FA Cup	Manchester United 2-1 Fulham	67,614
28/02/04	League	Fulham 1-1 Manchester United	18,306
25/10/03	League	Manchester United 1-3 Fulham	67,727

ALL-TIME RECORD VS FULHAM

Played	Won	Drawn	Lost	For	Against
59	33	15	11	109	68

GOAL BREAKDOWN 2004/05

Time (mins)	For	Against
0-15	6 (10%)	3 (12%)
16-30	7 (12%)	4 (15%)
31-45	9 (16%)	2 (8%)
46-60	11 (19%)	8 (31%)
61-75	12 (21%)	6 (23%)
76-90+	13 (22%)	3 (12%)

USEFUL INFORMATION

Nickname	The Red Devils
Manager	Sir Alex Ferguson
Chairman	TBC
Telephone	0870 442 1994
Ticket Office	0870 442 1999
Club Shop	0870 111 8107
Website	www.manutd.com

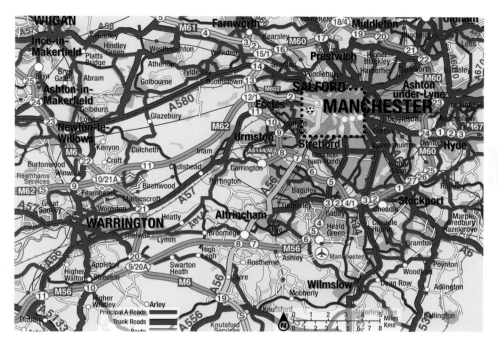

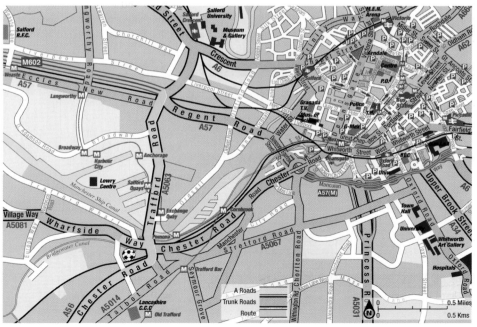

Middlesbrough

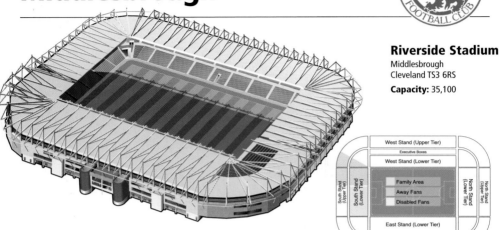

Riverside Stadium
Middlesbrough
Cleveland TS3 6RS
Capacity: 35,100

| West Stand (Upper Tier) |
| Executive Boxes |
| West Stand (Lower Tier) |
| Family Area / Away Fans / Disabled Fans |
| East Stand (Lower Tier) |
| East Stand (Upper Tier) |

Season Review 2004/05

Middlesbrough enjoyed some memorable European encounters, most notably a 2-0 victory against Lazio at the Riverside Stadium, and booked a second consecutive season of UEFA Cup football by finishing seventh in the Premiership. New boy Jimmy Floyd Hasselbaink weighed in with 13 League goals, while left-winger Stewart Downing was handed an England debut on the way to registering 14 top-flight assists.

FINAL POSITION 2004/05

	P	W	D	L	F	A	GD	Pts
06 Bolton Wanderers	38	16	10	12	49	44	5	58
07 Middlesbrough	38	14	13	11	53	46	7	55
08 Manchester City	38	13	13	12	47	39	8	52

RECENT MEETINGS

Date	Competition	Result	Attendance
19/04/05	League	Middlesbrough 1-1 Fulham	30,650
25/08/04	League	Fulham 0-2 Middlesbrough	17,759
07/01/04	League	Middlesbrough 2-1 Fulham	27,869
16/08/03	League	Fulham 3-2 Middlesbrough	14,546
19/01/03	League	Fulham 1-0 Middlesbrough	14,253

ALL-TIME RECORD VS FULHAM

Played	Won	Drawn	Lost	For	Against
48	22	7	19	81	66

GOAL BREAKDOWN 2004/05

Time (mins)	For	Against
0-15	3 (6%)	7 (15%)
16-30	6 (11%)	3 (7%)
31-45	11 (21%)	6 (13%)
46-60	14 (26%)	9 (20%)
61-75	7 (13%)	7 (15%)
76-90+	12 (23%)	14 (30%)

USEFUL INFORMATION

Nickname	Boro
Manager	Steve McClaren
Chairman	Steve Gibson
Telephone	0870 421 1986
Ticket Office	0870 421 1986
Club Shop	0870 421 1986
Website	www.mfc.co.uk

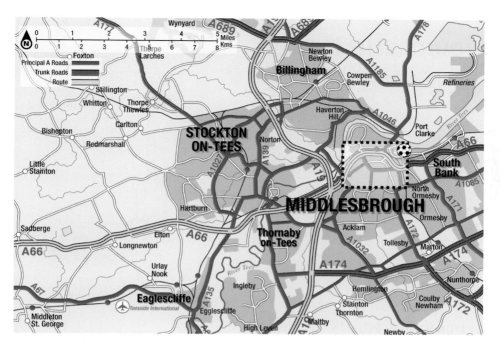

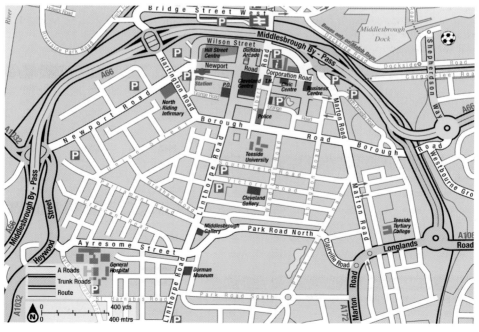

Newcastle United

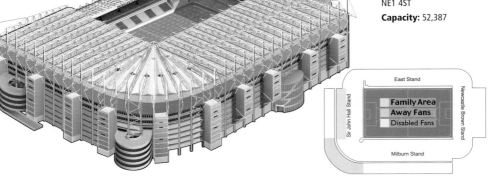

St James' Park
Newcastle-upon-Tyne
NE1 4ST
Capacity: 52,387

East Stand

Family Area
Away Fans
Disabled Fans

Sir John Hall Stand

Newcastle Brown Stand

Milburn Stand

Season Review 2004/05

There was never a dull moment at St James' Park last season, though this had little to do with football. The problems began after Sir Bobby Robson was replaced by Graeme Souness. Craig Bellamy branded his manager a "liar" and was loaned to Celtic, while Lee Bowyer and Kieron Dyer started fighting each other on the pitch during a game with Aston Villa.

Fulham were 4-1 winners in the North East, despite Newcastle managing 26 attempts at goal.

FINAL POSITION 2004/05

	P	W	D	L	F	A	GD	Pts
13 Fulham	38	12	8	18	52	60	-8	44
14 Newcastle United	38	10	14	14	47	57	-10	44
15 Blackburn Rovers	38	9	15	14	32	43	-11	42

RECENT MEETINGS

Date	Competition	Result	Attendance
04/05/05	League	Fulham 1-3 Newcastle United	19,003
07/11/04	League	Newcastle United 1-4 Fulham	51,118
19/01/04	League	Newcastle United 3-1 Fulham	50,104
21/10/03	League	Fulham 2-3 Newcastle United	16,506
19/04/03	League	Fulham 2-1 Newcastle United	17,900

ALL-TIME RECORD VS FULHAM

Played	Won	Drawn	Lost	For	Against
53	22	11	20	106	89

GOAL BREAKDOWN 2004/05

Time (mins)	For	Against
0-15	9 (19%)	3 (5%)
16-30	4 (9%)	5 (9%)
31-45	11 (23%)	9 (16%)
46-60	6 (13%)	13 (23%)
61-75	8 (17%)	16 (28%)
76-90+	9 (19%)	11 (19%)

USEFUL INFORMATION

Nickname	The Magpies
Manager	Graeme Souness
Chairman	Freddy Shepherd
Telephone	01912 018 400
Ticket Office	01912 611 571
Club Shop	01912 018 426
Website	www.nufc.co.uk

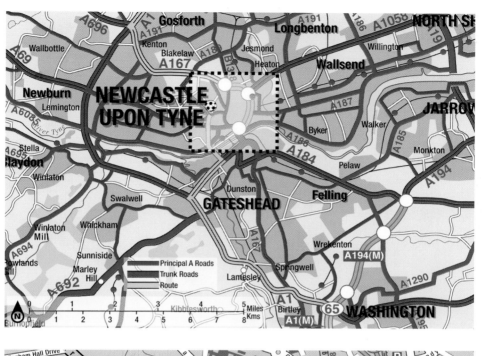

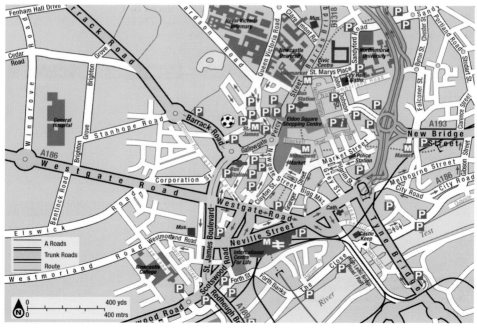

Portsmouth

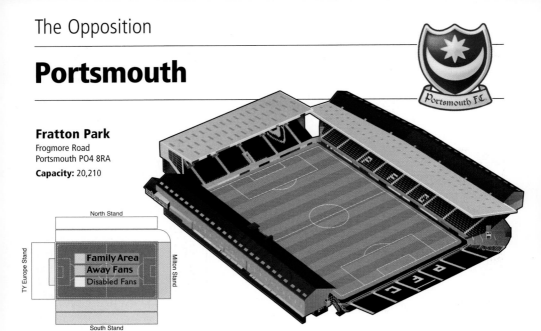

Fratton Park
Frogmore Road
Portsmouth PO4 8RA
Capacity: 20,210

Season Review 2004/05

It was a season of managerial uncertainty on the South Coast, with Harry Redknapp, Velimir Zajec and, eventually, Alain Perrin taking charge.

Portsmouth struggled for consistency, often following a good win with a poor defeat. A terrible run of just five points from 12 games after Christmas – culminating in a 3-1 reverse at Craven Cottage – saw Perrin arrive sooner than expected to guide the team to Premiership safety.

FINAL POSITION 2004/05

	P	W	D	L	F	A	GD	Pts
15 Blackburn Rovers	38	9	15	14	32	43	-11	42
16 Portsmouth	38	10	9	19	43	59	-16	39
17 West Bromwich Albion	38	6	16	16	36	61	-25	34

GOAL BREAKDOWN 2004/05

Time (mins)	For	Against
0-15	6 (14%)	10 (17%)
16-30	11 (26%)	10 (17%)
31-45	8 (19%)	12 (20%)
46-60	5 (12%)	4 (7%)
61-75	7 (16%)	11 (19%)
76-90+	6 (14%)	12 (20%)

RECENT MEETINGS

Date	Competition	Result	Attendance
03/04/05	League	Fulham 3-1 Portsmouth	20,502
30/08/04	League	Portsmouth 4-3 Fulham	19,728
01/05/04	League	Portsmouth 1-1 Fulham	20,065
24/11/03	League	Fulham 2-0 Portsmouth	15,624
21/04/01	League	Portsmouth 1-1 Fulham	17,651

USEFUL INFORMATION

Nickname	Pompey
Manager	Alain Perrin
Chairman	Milan Mandaric
Telephone	02392 731 204
Ticket Office	0871 230 1898
Club Shop	02392 838 238
Website	www.pompeyfc.co.uk

ALL-TIME RECORD VS FULHAM

Played	Won	Drawn	Lost	For	Against
45	20	15	10	69	49

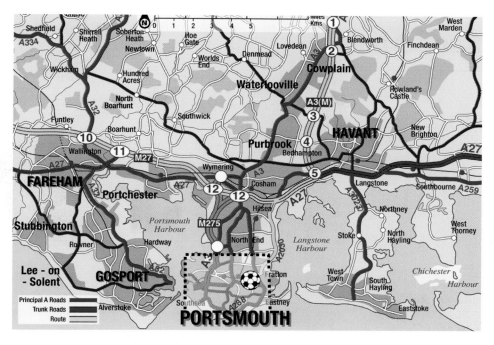

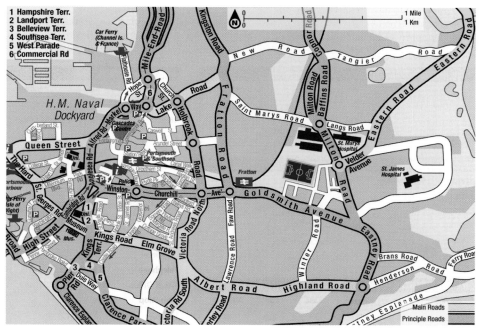

1 Hampshire Terr.
2 Landport Terr.
3 Belleview Terr.
4 Southsea Terr.
5 West Parade
6 Commercial Rd

The Opposition

Sunderland

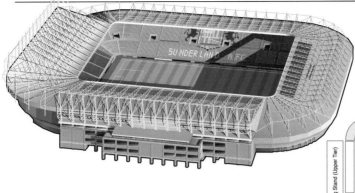

Stadium of Light
Sunderland SR5 1SU
Capacity: 48,300

Foster's Stand (Upper Tier)
Foster's Stand (Lower Tier)
Family Area
Away Fans
Disabled Fans
West Stand (Lower Tier)
West Stand (Upper Tier)

Season Review 2004/05

Sunderland won the inaugural Coca-Cola Championship, despite not occupying top-spot until early March.

The Black Cats timed their surge up the table to perfection, winning 11 of their final 13 games to finish seven points clear of runners-up Wigan.

Success owed much to manager Mick McCarthy's transfer dealings, as the former Republic of Ireland boss took a chance on players from the lower leagues, such as Dean Whitehead and Liam Lawrence.

FINAL POSITION 2004/05 (CHAMPIONSHIP)

	P	W	D	L	F	A	GD	Pts
01 Sunderland	46	29	7	10	76	41	35	94
02 Wigan Athletic	46	25	12	9	79	35	44	87
03 Ipswich Town	46	24	13	9	85	56	29	85

GOAL BREAKDOWN 2004/05

Time (mins)	For	Against
0-15	8 (11%)	8 (20%)
16-30	8 (11%)	6 (15%)
31-45	11 (14%)	9 (22%)
46-60	14 (18%)	2 (5%)
61-75	19 (25%)	4 (10%)
76-90+	16 (21%)	12 (29%)

RECENT MEETINGS

Date	Competition	Result	Attendance
01/03/03	League	Fulham 1-0 Sunderland	16,286
14/09/02	League	Sunderland 0-3 Fulham	35,432
19/01/02	League	Sunderland 1-1 Fulham	45,124
22/08/01	League	Fulham 2-0 Sunderland	20,197
03/10/89	League Cup	Fulham 0-3 Sunderland	Unknown

USEFUL INFORMATION

Nickname	The Black Cats
Manager	Mick McCarthy
Chairman	Bob Murray
Telephone	01915 515 000
Ticket Office	01915 515 151
Club Shop	01915 515 050
Website	www.safc.com

ALL-TIME RECORD VS FULHAM

Played	Won	Drawn	Lost	For	Against
44	19	12	13	66	58

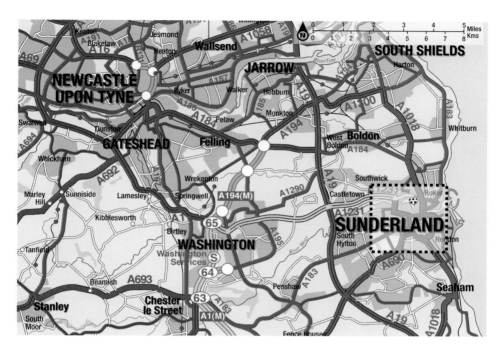

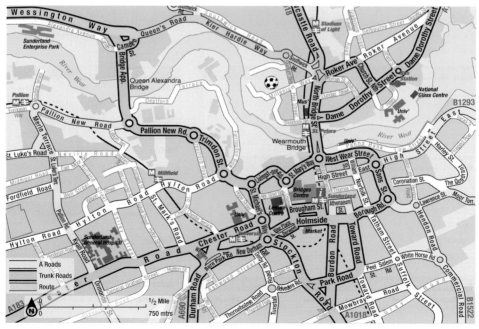

Tottenham Hotspur

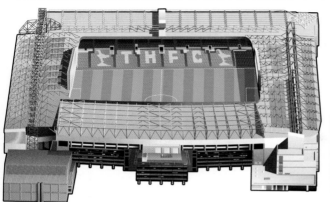

White Hart Lane

Bill Nicholson Way
748 High Road
London N17 0AP

Capacity: 36,214

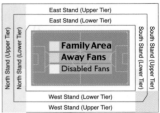

Season Review 2004/05

Following the brief and uninspiring reign of Frenchman Jacques Santini, Spurs fans were treated to a season of good football. Though Martin Jol's side finished just outside the UEFA Cup places in ninth spot, the policy of buying hungry young players such as Andy Reid and Michael Dawson gave reason for optimism. Tottenham impressed at White Hart Lane, scoring five goals in a match on three separate occasions.

FINAL POSITION 2004/05

	P	W	D	L	F	A	GD	Pts
08 Manchester City	38	13	13	12	47	39	8	52
09 Tottenham Hotspur	38	14	10	14	47	41	6	52
10 Aston Villa	38	12	11	15	45	52	-7	47

GOAL BREAKDOWN 2004/05

Time (mins)	For	Against
0-15	3 (6%)	4 (10%)
16-30	6 (13%)	4 (10%)
31-45	7 (15%)	10 (24%)
46-60	11 (23%)	7 (17%)
61-75	9 (19%)	8 (20%)
76-90+	11 (23%)	8 (20%)

RECENT MEETINGS

Date	Competition	Result	Attendance
26/02/05	League	Tottenham Hotspur 2-0 Fulham	35,885
30/10/04	League	Fulham 2-0 Tottenham Hotspur	21,317
31/01/04	League	Fulham 2-1 Tottenham Hotspur	17,024
30/08/03	League	Tottenham Hotspur 0-3 Fulham	33,421
24/02/03	League	Tottenham Hotspur 1-1 Fulham	34,704

USEFUL INFORMATION

Nickname	Spurs
Manager	Martin Jol
Chairman	Daniel Levy
Telephone	020 8365 5000
Ticket Office	0870 420 5000
Club Shop	020 8804 7888
Website	www.spurs.co.uk

ALL-TIME RECORD VS FULHAM

Played	Won	Drawn	Lost	For	Against
59	30	20	9	100	65

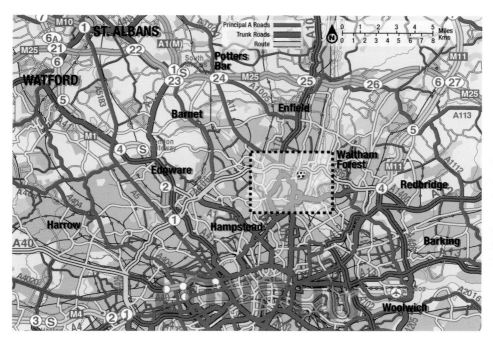

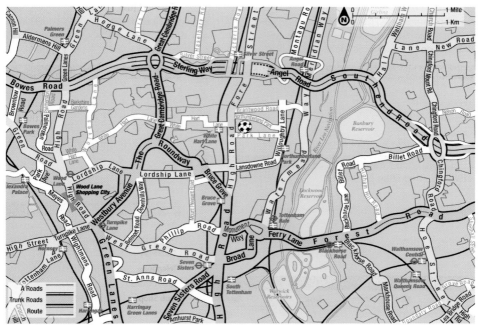

West Bromwich Albion

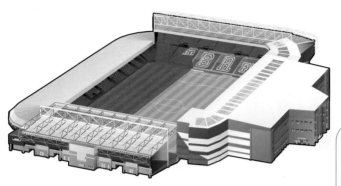

The Hawthorns
West Bromwich
West Midlands B71 4LF
Capacity: 28,003

Season Review 2004/05

Bryan Robson arrived at West Brom in November with his managerial reputation at rock-bottom. By the middle of May the former England captain was on top of the world, having guided a team propping up the Premiership at Christmas to survival. The astute acquisitions of Kevin Campbell and Kieran Richardson played their part, but it was the spirit created inside the camp that helped the Baggies climb three places to safety on the final afternoon.

FINAL POSITION 2004/05

	P	W	D	L	F	A	GD	Pts
16 Portsmouth	38	10	9	19	43	59	-16	39
17 West Bromwich Albion	38	6	16	16	36	61	-25	34
18 Crystal Palace	38	7	12	19	41	62	-21	33

GOAL BREAKDOWN 2004/05

Time (mins)	For	Against
0-15	6 (17%)	5 (8%)
16-30	2 (6%)	11 (18%)
31-45	7 (19%)	9 (15%)
46-60	5 (14%)	11 (18%)
61-75	6 (17%)	9 (15%)
76-90+	10 (28%)	16 (26%)

RECENT MEETINGS

Date	Competition	Result	Attendance
16/01/05	League	Fulham 1-0 West Brom	16,180
18/09/04	League	West Brom 1-1 Fulham	24,128
19/02/03	League	Fulham 3-0 West Brom	15,799
31/08/02	League	West Brom 1-0 Fulham	25,461
10/03/02	FA Cup	West Brom 0-1 Fulham	24,811

USEFUL INFORMATION

Nickname	The Baggies
Manager	Bryan Robson
Chairman	Jeremy Peace
Telephone	0870 066 8888
Ticket Office	0870 066 2800
Club Shop	0870 066 2810
Website	www.wba.co.uk

ALL-TIME RECORD VS FULHAM

Played	Won	Drawn	Lost	For	Against
69	33	14	22	112	80

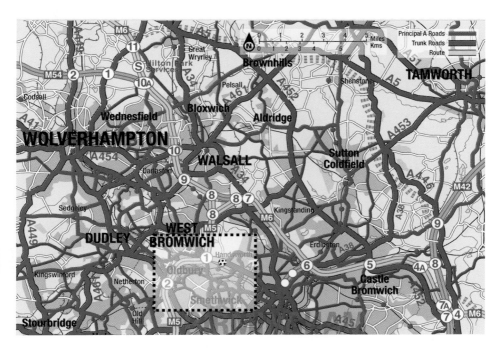

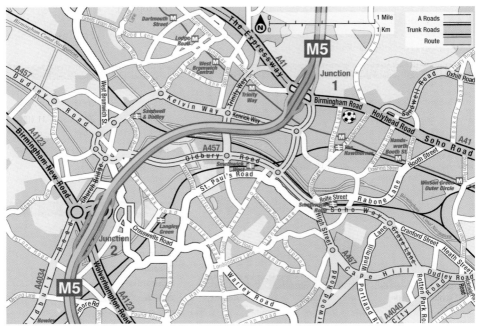

West Ham United

Boleyn Ground

Green Street
Upton Park
London E13 9AZ
Capacity: 35,647

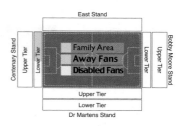

Season Review 2004/05

Having suffered heartbreak at the Millennium Stadium 12 months earlier, West Ham experienced the opposite emotion this time around.

The Hammers booked the final Play-Off place on the last day of the season, then beat Preston 1-0 in Cardiff after once again seeing off Ipswich at the Semi-Final stage.

Victory was sweet for heavily-criticised manager Alan Pardew, though he still has work to do to win over many of his own fans.

FINAL POSITION 2004/05 (CHAMPIONSHIP)

	P	W	D	L	F	A	GD	Pts
05 Preston North End	46	21	12	13	67	58	9	75
06 West Ham United	46	21	10	15	66	56	10	73
07 Reading	46	19	13	14	51	44	7	70

RECENT MEETINGS

Date	Competition	Result	Attendance
24/02/04	FA Cup	West Ham United 0-3 Fulham	27,934
14/02/04	FA Cup	Fulham 0-0 West Ham United	14,705
26/12/02	League	West Ham United 1-1 Fulham	35,025
23/10/02	League	Fulham 0-1 West Ham United	15,858
01/04/02	League	Fulham 0-1 West Ham United	19,416

ALL-TIME RECORD VS FULHAM

Played	Won	Drawn	Lost	For	Against
73	30	16	27	112	108

GOAL BREAKDOWN 2004/05

Time (mins)	For	Against
0-15	7 (11%)	9 (16%)
16-30	11 (17%)	7 (13%)
31-45	11 (17%)	8 (14%)
46-60	9 (14%)	10 (18%)
61-75	10 (15%)	8 (14%)
76-90+	18 (27%)	14 (25%)

USEFUL INFORMATION

Nickname	The Hammers
Manager	Alan Pardew
Chairman	Terence Brown
Telephone	020 8548 2748
Ticket Office	0870 112 2700
Club Shop	020 8548 4453
Website	www.whufc.com

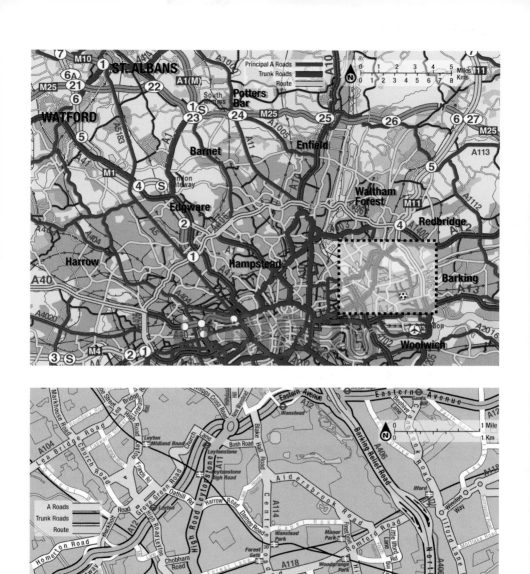

Wigan Athletic

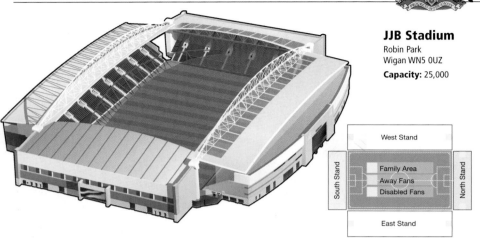

JJB Stadium
Robin Park
Wigan WN5 0UZ
Capacity: 25,000

West Stand

South Stand

Family Area
Away Fans
Disabled Fans

North Stand

East Stand

Season Review 2004/05

With the financial backing of Dave Whelan and the managerial nous of Paul Jewell behind them, Wigan clinched a place in the top-flight of English football for the first time in their history.

The Latics were in the top two for almost the entire campaign, with strikers Jason Roberts and Nathan Ellington contributing 45 League goals between them. It was fitting that both men scored in the 3-1 final-day win against Reading that secured promotion.

FINAL POSITION 2004/05 (CHAMPIONSHIP)

	P	W	D	L	F	A	GD	Pts
01 Sunderland	46	29	7	10	76	41	35	94
02 Wigan Athletic	46	25	12	9	79	35	44	87
03 Ipswich Town	46	24	13	9	85	56	29	85

RECENT MEETINGS

Date	Competition	Result	Attendance
23/09/03	League Cup	Wigan Athletic 1-0 Fulham	4,874
04/12/02	League Cup	Wigan Athletic 2-1 Fulham	7,615
10/04/99	League	Fulham 2-0 Wigan Athletic	12,140
01/12/98	League	Wigan Athletic 2-0 Fulham	3,951
21/02/98	League	Fulham 2-0 Wigan Athletic	7,791

ALL-TIME RECORD VS FULHAM

Played	Won	Drawn	Lost	For	Against
26	8	7	11	27	36

GOAL BREAKDOWN 2004/05

Time (mins)	For	Against
0-15	9 (11%)	3 (9%)
16-30	20 (25%)	4 (11%)
31-45	8 (10%)	7 (20%)
46-60	19 (24%)	4 (11%)
61-75	11 (14%)	8 (23%)
76-90+	12 (15%)	9 (26%)

USEFUL INFORMATION

Nickname	The Latics
Manager	Paul Jewell
Chairman	Dave Whelan
Telephone	01942 770 460
Ticket Office	0870 1122 552
Club Shop	01942 212 122
Website	www.wiganlatics.co.uk

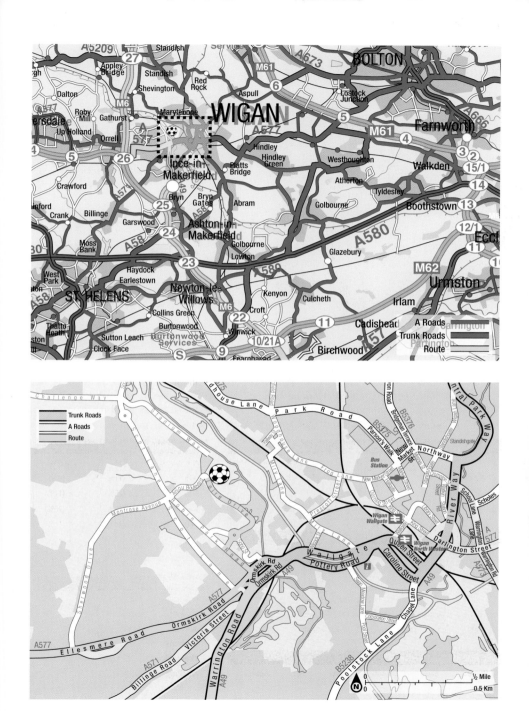

Barclays Premiership 2005-06 | Premiership history

Legend: ■ won ■ drawn ■ lost □ not played

Date	Team	Home/Away	04-05	Played	Goals for	Goals against	Scored first	Best result	Worst
13.08.05	Birmingham	H	2-3	3	2	4	0	0-0	2-3
20.08.05	Blackburn	A	3-1	4	6	6	1	3-1	0-3
24.08.05	Arsenal	A	0-2	4	2	8	0	0-0	1-4
27.08.05	Everton	H	2-0	4	8	1	4	2-0	2-1
10.09.05	Newcastle	A	4-1	4	6	7	1	4-1	1-3
17.09.05	West Ham	H	N/A	2	0	2	0	0-1	0-1
26.09.05	Tottenham	A	0-2	4	4	7	2	3-0	0-4
01.10.05	Man Utd	H	1-1	4	5	6	1	1-1	2-3
17.10.05	Charlton	A	1-2	4	4	6	1	1-0	1-3
22.10.05	Liverpool	H	2-4	4	6	10	2	3-2	2-4
29.10.05	Wigan	A	N/A	0	0	0	0	N/A	N/A
05.11.05	Man City	H	1-1	3	3	4	0	2-2	0-1
20.11.05	Middlesbro	A	1-1	4	5	7	1	2-2	1-2
26.11.05	Bolton	H	2-0	4	11	2	2	4-1	2-1
03.12.05	West Brom	A	1-1	2	1	2	1	1-1	0-1
10.12.05	Birmingham	A	2-1	3	4	3	1	2-1	2-2
17.12.05	Blackburn	H	0-2	4	5	10	1	2-0	0-4
26.12.05	Chelsea	A	1-3	4	5	9	0	1-1	1-3
28.12.05	Aston Villa	H	1-1	4	4	4	1	2-1	1-2
31.12.05	Portsmouth	A	3-4	2	4	5	0	1-1	3-4
02.01.06	Sunderland	H	N/A	2	3	0	2	2-0	1-0
14.01.06	Newcastle	H	1-3	4	8	8	2	3-1	1-3
21.01.06	West Ham	A	N/A	2	3	1	2	2-0	1-1
01.02.06	Tottenham	H	2-0	4	7	5	1	2-0	0-2
04.02.06	Man Utd	A	0-1	4	5	8	2	3-1	0-3
11.02.06	West Brom	H	1-0	2	4	0	2	3-0	1-0
25.02.06	Bolton	A	1-3	4	3	3	1	2-0	1-3
04.03.06	Arsenal	H	0-3	4	1	8	0	0-1	0-3
11.03.06	Everton	A	0-1	4	2	8	0	1-2	1-3
18.03.06	Chelsea	H	1-4	4	2	6	0	1-1	1-4
25.03.06	Aston Villa	A	0-2	4	1	10	0	1-3	0-3
01.04.06	Portsmouth	H	3-1	2	5	1	1	3-1	3-1
08.04.06	Sunderland	A	N/A	2	4	1	2	3-0	1-1
15.04.06	Charlton	H	0-0	4	3	0	1	2-0	0-0
17.04.06	Liverpool	A	1-3	4	1	5	0	0-0	1-3
22.04.06	Wigan	H	N/A	0	0	0	0	N/A	N/A
29.04.06	Man City	A	1-1	3	2	5	1	1-1	1-4
07.05.06	Middlesbro	H	0-2	4	6	5	1	3-2	0-2